WINNING
BIG
With BARGAIN STOCKS

WINNING
BIG
With BARGAIN STOCKS

HOW TO INVEST SUCCESSFULLY IN NEW
ISSUES, WARRANTS, AND STOCKS OF
TURNAROUND COMPANIES UNDER $10

BILL MATHEWS

Dearborn
Financial Publishing, Inc.

While a great deal of care has been taken to provide accurate and current information, the ideas, suggestions, general principles and conclusions presented in this book are subject to local, state and federal laws and regulations, court cases and any revisions of same. The reader is thus urged to consult legal counsel regarding any points of law—this publication should not be used as a substitute for competent legal advice.

Publisher: Kathleen A. Welton
Associate Editor: Karen A. Christensen
Project Editors: Linda S. Miller/Jack L. Kiburz
Interior Design: Mary Kushmir

Published by Dearborn Financial Publishing Inc.

Printed in the United States of America

92 93 10 9 8 7 6 5 4 3 2

Library of Congress Cataloging-in-Publication Data

Mathews, Bill.
    Winning big with bargain stocks: how to invest successfully in new issues, warrants, and stocks of turnaround companies under $10/by Bill Mathews.
        p. cm.
    Includes bibliographical references and index.
    ISBN 0-79310-268-5: $19.95
    1. Investments—United States—Handbooks, manuals, etc.
    2. Stocks—United States—Handbooks, manuals, etc. I. Title.
HG4921.M35   1991
332.63'22—dc20   91-13009
                                                                         CIP

CONTENTS

PREFACE

Since August of 1981 when I started publishing my investment newsletter, *The CHEAP Investor*, I have witnessed both good and bad markets. However, because of the major stock-market crash on October 19, 1987, many small investors have been afraid to invest in the market and have missed some great bargains. The Middle East oil crisis in 1990 severely shook the little confidence that they had in common stocks.

As repercussions from these crashes have continued to affect investors, many quality, low-priced stocks have become extremely undervalued. I developed this book to teach the small investor how to choose wisely from the cornucopia of bargain stocks to reap huge profits.

The main goal of *Winning Big with Bargain Stocks* is simply to help you become the *best* investor you can be. Statistics indicate that 70 percent of all investors lose money in the stock market. Why? Most investors buy poor-quality stocks at too high a price and either they become greedy and don't take their profits or they ignore signals that indicate the price may go down and end up selling their stock for a loss.

This book will give you a better understanding of the stock market in general: it will explain how to choose quality stocks, how to buy them at a good price and when to sell them for a tidy profit. It also will explain why you should specialize in one area and learn it well and how you can avoid stock scams.

Winning Big with Bargain Stocks is an expanded version of the college course that I have taught and refined for the past 15 years. The book contains practical advice on investing in bargain stocks and offers numerous examples. You can study it in your leisure at your own pace to learn the ins and outs of investing in bargain stocks. I am sure this will be a convenient reference book that you will use again and again.

This book was written in easy-to-understand language in a format that moves from the basics into more specific concepts. It is designed to help you learn the essential information that you need to make an educated judgment on the value of an investment.

It also shows you how to test your stock-analysis abilities without risking any money. Once you are convinced that you have learned how to make wiser investment decisions, you can move on to the excitement of investing your money in stocks that you know have the potential for producing good-sized profits.

By purchasing this book, you have taken the first step to becoming a better investor. Now make sure that you spend the necessary time to receive the most benefit from it. Let *Winning Big with Bargain Stocks* be your guide to following your investment dream to huge profits.

I welcome your comments on the book and hope you find it interesting, educational and most of all profitable.

Bill Mathews, Editor
Mathews and Associates, Inc.
2549 West Golf Road, Suite 350
Hoffman Estates, IL 60194

CHAPTER

1

Following Your Investment Dream

Knowledge is power. If an investor is knowledgeable about a stock, he or she will be able to make an educated decision on whether or not to purchase it. The investor will not have to rely on anyone else who may or may not be more interested in a commission than in the quality of the investment. This book will provide you with all the necessary information to analyze a stock on your own, to realize what is a good price to purchase the stock, to recognize when to take your profit and to learn how to protect your profits.

YOUR FIRST STEPS BEFORE CONSIDERING ANY INVESTMENT

Almost 50 million Americans from all walks of life own stock in U.S. businesses. Making money from buying and selling stocks is an exciting proposition; before you begin, however, you must ask yourself if you are ready to invest.

You don't need to earn $100,000 a year to invest. In fact, a survey by the New York Stock Exchange found that approximately 34 percent of all shareholders had annual incomes of only $25,000 or less. However, you should take a hard look at your financial situation. Your income should cover your basic expenses and you should set up an emergency fund equal to six months' salary. Once you have made sure that you are financially secure, then your remaining funds can be invested. Any investment involves some degree of risk, so the funds you have earmarked should be money that you can afford to lose.

After you have decided to invest your extra cash, you should analyze just what you want to accomplish through the investments. Your individual situation should guide you. If you are near retirement or already living on a fixed income, then your investing program should be designed to earn dividends or interest while protecting your principal.

If you receive more income from various sources or if you are young enough that you believe you can take more risks with your capital, then investing in quality, low-priced stocks can be just right for you. If you have ample capital, you should consider diversifying. You can place part of your capital in a program with a lower, but more secure return and then invest the balance in quality bargain (or CHEAP) stocks with a greater profit potential.

THE CHEAP PHILOSOPHY APPROACH
TO INVESTING

Originally, the CHEAP philosophy was developed in response to my personal investment experiences. After a decade and a half of teaching college-level investment courses, I have tested, modified and perfected the philosophy. It has become the cornerstone of my newsletter, *The CHEAP Investor*, which has been successfully utilized by tens of thousands of investors across the country.

My introduction to investing occurred during the late 1960s when my broker recommended buying AT&T because, according to him, it was the highest-quality blue-chip stock and would therefore be my best investment. At that time, AT&T was the most profitable company in the country and its stock was selling at $63 per share. As an avid admirer of the automobile industry, I also became interested in American Motors, which was producing several very innovative and exciting cars. When I called my broker to buy some American Motors stock, he tried to persuade me to give up the foolish notion, claiming that the company was on the verge of bankruptcy for it had just set a new record for the largest loss suffered by any company.

When my broker realized that he couldn't talk me out of my "crazy" idea, he asked me to sign a statement indicating that he had not recommended buying the $3 stock. I signed the statement and he bought the stock. While I invested the same amount of money in American Motors that I did in AT&T, because it was only $3 compared to $63, I received 21 times as many shares of American Motors.

Six months later, AT&T dropped from $63 to $48 or −24 percent while American Motors rose from $3 to $13 or +333 percent! It didn't matter that AT&T was the most profitable and recognized blue chip and that American Motors had experienced the largest loss in history. I learned a valuable lesson—one that changed my life forever. From that point on, I always questioned investing in a company just because it was a blue chip. While I didn't know what a turnaround stock was when I invested in American Motors, I soon learned and used that knowledge.

Another episode changed my view of investing. A neighbor of mine worked for S. S. Kresge and one day he was complaining to me that he had an option but no money to buy 11 shares of the stock at $33 per share (a 20 percent discount on its market price). I had some extra money, so I offered him ten percent of the profits if he let me use the option to buy those 11 shares for $363. Over the next year, S. S. Kresge's stock moved up to $99 and split three for one, giving us 33 shares at $33 each. Over the next two years, it again reached $99 and split three for one. Now we had 99 shares at $33 or $3,267. The stock continued to move upward and a couple years later we sold out at $62 for $6,138. In a little more than five years, we had parlayed a $363 investment to more than $6,000.

Why did the stock soar? While you may not recognize the name S. S. Kresge, you probably recognize its creation, K Mart, which changed the retailing industry. When I originally bought the stock, the company had produced tremendous increases in sales and earnings and its stock moved up accordingly. During that same time period, Sears, the world's largest retailer, experienced only a slight increase in its stock price. I learned that I was wiser to invest in a smaller company with good growth potential than in a mature industry leader.

As I continued to develop my investment philosophy, I realized that much of my success was accomplished by acting contrary to the recommendations of Wall Street and the media. In essence, I became a successful investor not by following the crowd, but by challenging it. These experiences, along with my teaching and research, formed the foundation of the CHEAP philosophy. The 12 rules that constitute the CHEAP philosophy are:

1. Become an educated investor. Let's face it, no one has as much interest as you do in seeing your money grow. Your best investment is to spend the time to become educated about the investing process so you can make intelligent investment decisions. You don't buy a house without checking it out. Why buy stocks without knowing anything about them? Becoming an educated investor will not only save you money in commissions, but should greatly increase your investing successes.

2. Invest in a company, not in a market. The market is only one factor determining whether a stock's price will go up or down. The major factor affecting the direction the company's stock will move is the quality of the company itself. If the company has increased its sales and earnings, the stock usually will move upward regardless of the market. However, if the company has experienced huge losses and decreased sales, its stock price normally will drop even if the market is moving upward.

3. Don't be a jack-of-all-trades and a master of none—specialize in one specific area. Learning everything about all types of investments is overwhelming. A way to reduce this to a more manageable load is to specialize in one area of investing. Becoming an educated investor in a specific area can prove extremely lucrative. My research shows that investors specializing in quality, low-priced stocks can far outpace the market.

4. Don't fall victim to the greed/fear trap. A pitfall that catches most investors at one time or another is the greed/fear trap. Greed enters into the picture when an investor has made a nice profit on a stock, but hesitates to take the profit because the investor believes he or she can get even more. When the stock price starts to fall, the investor becomes afraid to sell because he or she assumes it will go up again and watches as the stock moves back down to or below the original purchase price.

5. Don't lose money by investing in the wrong price stocks. When investors purchase higher-priced stocks, they encounter two obstacles to successful investing. The first is they can't afford to buy as many shares so commission fees can wipe out a major portion of the profit. The second is many higher-priced stocks are so expensive that it is almost mathematically impossible for them to double in price. They have already experienced their major growth.

6. To make profits, carefully consider the number of shares you control. Commissions for 1,000 shares of stock may cost only two or three times the price for 100 shares. This can directly affect your profit. In addition, if you bought 100 shares of a $30 stock and 1,000 shares of a $3, if both went up $1, the $30 stock would realize a $100 profit, while the $3 stock would experience a $1,000 profit.

7. Always look at profits and losses in percentages, not in points.
How would you have profited if the $30 stock goes up $5 and the $3
stock only rises $1? Offhand, you may say the $30 stock performed better. However, if you actually figure out the profit percentage, you would
see that the $30 stock moved up 16.7 percent while the $3 stock rose 33.3
percent!

**8. Consider the purchase price of a stock to determine your
profit.** Most stocks are cyclical. This means they go up near their 52-
week high and then down near the 52-week low and then back up again.
If you buy a stock near its 52-week high, the law of averages is against
you. It is much smarter to buy a quality stock near its 52-week low
where it has greater profit potential.

9. Being patient can pay off in profits. It takes patience to wait for
a stock to dip near its 52-week-low price, but this can mean the difference between a profit or a loss. Many times I have followed a stock for a
year or more before it achieved the perfect combination of being a high-
quality company at a low price.

**10. Buy your stock when no one wants it and sell it when every-
one wants to buy.** If you invest contrary to the masses, you will be able
to buy the stock while there is little demand for it and the price is low.
Likewise, when other investors are clamoring to buy the stock and its
price goes up, you already have made a nice profit and can sell while others are buying at a much higher price.

11. Don't take anyone else's word; investigate before you invest.
Many times an investor is so blinded by greed that he or she forgets to
ask any questions about the investment. Letting someone else make
your investment decisions certainly is easier, yet it makes you more susceptible to high-pressure scam artists. Telephone scam artists pressure
you to buy right away without thinking it over. Never buy any investment without getting information *in writing* so you can analyze it. Doing
so can save a lot of money and trouble.

**12. Follow your stock price so you do not miss major profit op-
portunities.** Many investors become lazy after they have purchased a
stock and don't follow its price. That can be their downfall. Some stocks
are very volatile and may double in price only to fall back a week or two
later. If the investor hasn't been watching the price, he or she may miss a
great opportunity for profit.

Perhaps the biggest eye opener for me was discovering that I could
make more profitable investments by choosing stocks myself rather than
by relying on a broker. To maintain my success, I realized that I had to
learn as much as possible about the stock to intelligently decide whether
or not it was a good investment.

☐   **RULE 1**   ☐

Become an educated investor.

Whenever your broker, friend or relative gives you a stock tip, don't immediately buy the stock without checking. Stop to think for a moment. Take the time to find out what the current stock price is. Is it near the stock's 52-week high or low price? The cardinal rule of investing is to buy a stock at a low price and sell it for a higher price. If the stock you are interested in is already at its historical high, your chances of making a profit are greatly reduced—so stay away from it. If the stock is near its 52-week low price, this is a great starting point. However, you must take the next step, which is to analyze the company.

Why do reasonable people who would never consider buying a car without checking to see if it is a good purchase blindly invest thousands of dollars in companies that basically have nothing to offer? I believe that most investors are intimidated by the overwhelming number of companies and types of investments. They figure that they would never be able to learn enough about these companies and investments so they must rely on experts. This is OK as long as the expert knows what he or she is doing. If the expert doesn't, the investor usually finds out only after he or she is several thousand dollars poorer.

WELCOME TO THE WORLD OF BARGAIN INVESTMENTS

The stock market can be mystifying to the novice. For example, just what does it mean when someone says a stock is at $11\frac{1}{8}$? Even though the stock price is sometimes referred to as points, it is translated into dollars so that $11\frac{1}{8}$ is actually 11 and $\frac{1}{8}$ dollars or $11.125. Why does the stock market use fractions such as $\frac{1}{8}$ or $\frac{1}{16}$ when our currency is based on tens? I believe that when the original stock market began during the 1700s, it was based on Spanish currency (remember pieces of eight?) and the exchange adopted that breakdown of the dollar. It is outdated, but don't hold your breath waiting for it to be changed. Instead, use Table 1.1 to convert the fractions into cents.

One of the basics of investing is following the company's stock price. Some stocks don't move very much and you may need to check them only once a week. However, it is a good idea to follow most stocks daily.

Table 1.1 Conversion of Fractions to Cents

Fraction	Cents	Fraction	Cents	Fraction	Cents	Fraction	Cents
1/32	$ .03125	9/32	$ .28125	17/32	$ .53125	25/32	$ .78125
1/16	.0625	5/16	.3125	9/16	.5625	13/16	.8125
3/32	.09375	11/32	.34375	19/32	.59375	27/32	.84375
1/8	.125	3/8	.375	5/8	.625	7/8	.875
5/32	.15625	13/32	.40625	21/32	.65625	29/32	.90625
3/16	.1875	7/16	.4375	11/16	.6875	15/16	.9375
7/32	.21875	15/32	.46875	23/32	.71875	31/32	.96875
1/4	.25	1/2	.50	3/4	.75	1	1.00

Sometimes fantastic news can cause a stock to rise or fall quickly in price and if you aren't watching, you may miss a profit opportunity.

You can call your broker every day; yet, it would be more courteous to check the stock price in *The Wall Street Journal,* the *Investor's Daily* or your local newspaper. Figure 1.1 shows the various column headings and what they mean.

The stock table for the over-the-counter (OTC) market is very similar to the listing in Figure 1.1 except that OTC stocks have a bid and asked price that may be listed. The bid price is what the shareholder would receive if he or she sold the stock and the asked price is what the shareholder would pay to buy the stock.

HOW INDIVIDUALS CAN EASILY OUTPACE THE MARKET

As you are looking for a stock to invest in, remember that your main concern is whether the company is a good investment, not if the market will go up or down.

Whenever you read about the market going up or down, have you wondered what it actually is referring to? Does it mean every stock on that particular market went up or down? Is it an average? These are good questions to keep in mind the next time you hear a newsperson on television solemnly reading, "The market is down 14 points." In most cases, the newsperson is referring to the Dow Jones Industrial index, which is comprised of 30 stocks. While these 30 stocks may have averaged an upward or downward movement, it is very possible that the stocks you have invested in have remained unchanged or have moved in the opposite direction.

Figure 1.1   Typical Newspaper Listing for a Stock on the NYSE and ASE

52-WEEK HIGH LOW	STOCKS	STOCK SYM.	DIV.	YLD. %	P. E. RATIO	SALES 100S	HIGH	LOW	CLOSE	NET CHANGE
6 3½	ECC INTL	ECC	.20	5	7	714	4⅝	3⅞	4	+ ¼
(A)	(B)	(C)	(D)	(E)	(F)	(G)	(H)	(I)	(J)	(K)

(A)	52-WEEK HIGH/LOW	The highest and the lowest price per share (high is $6 per share, low is $3.50 per share) that this stock has traded for during the past 52 weeks.
(B)	STOCKS	The name of the stock. In this case, it is ECC International.
(C)	STOCK SYMBOL	The group of letters assigned to a stock allowing a broker to access the stock on his or her computer to check the price and other information.
(D)	DIV.	The annual cash dividend paid on the stock. ECC paid $ .20 per share.
(E)	YLD. %	The dividend in terms of yield percent. Because there is a $ .20 dividend and the close of the stock is $4, the yield percent is 5.
(F)	P. E. RATIO	The price-earnings ratio for this stock is 7. The previous day's closing price divided by the latest 12-month per share earnings for the company becomes the P. E. Ratio. This is used to measure comparative values among different stocks. If there is no P. E. Ratio, then the company is not making money; if there is a P. E. Ratio, then the company is profitable.
(G)	SALES 100S	The day's trading volume of this stock. The number 714 is in hundreds of shares. Therefore, a total of 71,400 shares was traded that day. (You must have both a buy and a sell transaction to constitute a trade.)
(H)	HIGH	The highest price ($4.625 per share) at which the stock was traded during the day.
(I)	LOW	The lowest price ($3.875 per share) at which the stock was traded during the day.
(J)	CLOSE	When the stock exchange bell rings and the market is closed, the last or "closing" price ($4 per share) for which the stock was traded.
(K)	NET CHANGE	The change in the closing price from the previous day's closing price. In this example, ECC was up 1/4 or $ .25 per share when compared to the previous day's closing price.

Figure 1.2 Price Cycle of Fonar Corporation

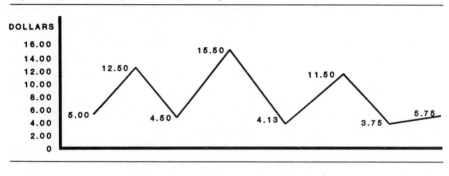

□ **RULE 2** □

Invest in a company, not in a market.

Many investors place too much emphasis on "what the market is doing" rather than on "does the company possess good profit potential." I strongly believe that a low-priced, quality stock has a good potential to make profits no matter what the market does. Market crashes such as the one in 1987 greatly affected the blue-chip stocks and caused panic that in turn affected the majority of lower-priced stocks. However, the crash didn't cause those quality low-priced companies to go out of business, and in most cases, their stock prices quickly rebounded.

From the middle of 1981 through most of 1987, the market kept moving higher and higher. During that time, IBM moved from $70 to a high of $175.88. Buying that stock and holding on to it would have resulted in a nice profit of 151 percent. However, I have found that a great number of stocks are cyclical. This means that their stock price goes up, comes down, goes up again, etc. By purchasing a quality stock that is near its 52-week low and selling it when it gets near its 52-week high, your profit potential is greatly multiplied.

Figure 1.2 shows the price cycle of Fonar Corporation. It displays four buy recommendations that I have given on the stock since October of 1981.

The lower figure is the price at which I recommended Fonar and the higher figure shows the highest price the stock hit after my recommendation. Obviously, buying and selling the stock would have given an investor some very nice profits. Because you have no way of knowing exactly what low and high price a stock will hit, it is best to buy near the low and sell when the stock price starts to back off from the high. For example, an investor spent $1,000 to buy 200 shares of Fonar at the originally recommended new-issue price of $5 and watched the stock rise to $12.50. When the stock price started to back off, he sold it at $10 and doubled his money to $2,000. If he continued to follow the stock and bought into it again at $5 the next time, he could purchase 400 shares with his $2,000. Once the stock started falling from the $15.50 high, even if he sold the stock for $12.50, the investor would have increased that initial $1,000 investment to $5,000.

By the way, if an investor had bought Fonar at the $5 new-issue price when I first recommended it and had just held on to it, she wouldn't be very happy right now since the stock is currently at $1 or down 80 percent.

For the past several years, many stocks have experienced smaller and more frequent price swings. In this type of market, if you have a stock that has risen 30, 40 or 50 percent, you should consider taking your profit before the price moves down again and you have lost the opportunity. As you can see, a good method for making money in this volatile market is to trade quality, low-priced cyclical stocks.

What should you do if you have sold your cyclical stock for a profit and then it continues to rise? You don't buy that stock at the much higher price hoping it will continue to go higher. This is a great way to lose money. Ideally, you should follow several cyclical investment candidates. Then you can invest your capital in one of the other stocks if it is at a good low price.

This chapter has given you some background to prepare you to master investing in bargain stocks. In Chapter 2, you will learn why common stocks are your best investment and why so many foreign investors buy U.S. stocks. Chapter 3 will teach you how the various exchanges work, how you buy or sell on the exchanges and why the Dow Jones Industrials index may be very misleading. Chapter 4 explains why companies sell stock and how you can become a better investor by specializing in one area. Chapter 5 shows you how to easily and profitably analyze stocks. Chapter 6 explains how the small investor can outpace the institutions by investing in stocks under $10.

Chapter 7 details the new-issue process and explains how to easily read a prospectus. Chapter 8 explains why companies go into bankruptcy and how you can profit from buying them when they are undervalued. Chapter 9 will show you how to make huge profits on turnaround stocks. Chapter 10 explains warrants and how to wisely buy them. Chapter 11 illustrates the difference between discount and full-service brokerage firms and helps you locate the best broker for your needs. Chapter 12 shows you how to buy stocks at the best price. Chapter 13 offers tips for selling for the best profits.

Chapter 14 teaches how economics can affect the stock market. Chapter 15 explains how you can profit from plummeting stock prices caused by major incidents such as the Middle East oil crisis or the 1987 stock market crash. Chapter 16 teaches you how to be a scamproof investor. Chapter 17 explains how you can apply what you have learned in simulated trading. Chapter 18 tests what you have learned. Also included is a glossary containing many of the important terms used by the investment industry.

So study this book to learn how you can best take advantage of bargain stocks.

CHAPTER

2

Why You Should Invest in Common Stocks

Recently, I read statistics indicating that Japan was number one in the amount of cash savings per individual, with an average of $40,000. The United States ranked number 11, with just $10,000 savings per individual. Many people were surprised by these statistics and wondered how the Japanese had been able to build their savings so quickly. While several factors entered into it, a big reason why they greatly increased their savings was investments in *common stock*. The Japanese invest as individuals and through their institutions, banks and pension funds. Americans, on the other hand, lost a tremendous amount of wealth during the 1980s. This occurred because small investors and institutions moved away from buying common stocks that create new jobs and instead invested in options, futures, certificates of deposit (CDs), junk bonds and other investments that do little to build economic growth.

Any individual can participate in our free-enterprise system by starting a company and becoming a direct owner. However, because most people don't have the necessary capital or entrepreneurial characteristics, they can indirectly share in the growth and prosperity of a company by investing in its common stock. An investor with a small amount of money can become a partial owner of a growing corporation and enjoy many of the same benefits as the entrepreneur.

This opportunity is available to everyone in our economic system. No wonder that more and more people are taking advantage of it and investing in common stocks. This chapter will help you understand what common stocks are and why you should invest in them.

Many foreign investors choose to buy U.S. common stocks instead of their own countries' stocks. Why? The United States is unique. Our political stability and the strength of our economy are unmatched and foreign investors are flocking to purchase U.S. common stocks because of their safety and their tremendous growth potential. The bottom line is that foreign investors can receive a better return from U.S. stocks.

Even if you have never called a broker and bought a common stock, you already may be investing in them through your pension fund, profit-sharing plan, mutual fund or other investment that you own. The major attraction of common stocks is that, over the long run, they outperform almost all other investments. They are easy to buy and sell, fairly simple to research and, most important of all, volatile with the potential for producing excellent profits.

WHAT IS A COMMON STOCK?

When you purchase common stock, you become a part owner of the company. The number of shares you buy determines your percentage of ownership in the firm. As a common-stock owner, you can share in the future of the company's earnings as well as vote (one vote per share) to decide on major issues affecting the company such as a merger. The ownership of common stock gives the investor a way of participating in the growth of virtually any corporation. In addition, owning common stock helps protect the investor against inflation, for over the years common stocks have far outpaced inflation.

Because thousands of companies offer shares of common stock, the investor has the opportunity to invest in a broad spectrum of industries. With virtually any investment, there is a risk that part or all of the investment may be lost. However, by investing in quality, low-priced stocks, the investor can greatly reduce the risk and increase the profit potential.

Basically, there are two ways to make money from common stock— either from dividends or from appreciation (from the sale of the stock after it increases from your purchase price). A stock only pays dividends when it is profitable. However, a stock's price can go up for many reasons. The stock price should move upward when:

1. The company has increased its sales and profits.
2. The company's industry is experiencing a boom period that may favorably affect the stock's price.

3. The company has announced a new product, acquisition or large sales contract.
4. The company is approached for a merger or a takeover (or there are rumors that this will be attempted).
5. A major Wall Street brokerage firm recommends buying the stock.

Of course, sometimes the company can announce tremendous news and the stock price stays the same or goes down. Likewise, the company can experience poor earnings or bad management or announce negative news and the stock price goes up. The stock price reaction is not always rational.

TYPES OF COMMON STOCKS

The term *common stock* is actually a generic name for several different categories of stocks. Sometimes a stock may fall into more than one category; for example, a company may be considered both a blue-chip and an income stock.

Blue-Chip Stocks

These are widely known companies with long histories of earnings and dividends. Blue chips are promoted by Wall Street as long-term, "safe" investments that, presumably, will offer a low-risk potential and will provide a modest return. IBM, General Motors, General Electric and the other well-known stocks listed on the Dow Jones indexes are considered blue-chip stocks.

The problem with blue-chip stocks is that they typically are extremely high priced ($60 and up) and the small investor can purchase only a few shares. Blue chips are huge, established companies that have already experienced a major period of growth. In my opinion, they offer the investor a small return on an overpriced stock. Blue-chip stocks are generally listed on the New York Stock Exchange (NYSE) and most of the time they follow the market on its upward and downward swings. However, because their stock prices are so high, these blue-chip stocks usually do not move up over 100 percent in a year.

Growth Stocks

Less well-known than blue chips, growth stocks still receive a good amount of publicity. They have enjoyed a several-year history of increasing sales and earnings and are promoted by Wall Street as good investments in a bull market. Because they are younger (10 to 25 years old) and smaller companies than the blue chips, they offer greater growth potential and usually grow faster than the economy and other companies in their industry. If a growth stock gives any dividend, it is very small. Apple, Compaq, AST Research, LA Gear, Waste Management and McDonald's are examples of growth companies.

Growth stocks normally range in price from $20 to $55, which means the small investor again can afford only a few shares. The stocks tend to be extremely volatile. Usually, they grow at higher percentages than blue-chip stocks, but they rely heavily on the health of the economy and their industry for that growth.

Income Stocks

These well-established companies have existed for a long time. They experience very small growth, normally about the same as the Gross National Product (GNP). However, the company returns most of its profits to the shareholder in the form of dividends. Income stocks tend to be high priced and Wall Street sells them as very "safe" investments. In many cases, the investor receives a dividend that barely covers inflation. AT&T, Commonwealth Edison and other utility stocks are regarded as income stocks and are not suited to an investor looking for growth.

Fad Stocks

These are usually created by Wall Street analysts in an industry that expands at a much greater rate than the GNP. Typically, a fad stock's price flies upward as investors jump on the bandwagon to buy. Because its price moves up so fast, the fad stock comes to the attention of more and more investors and they buy at higher and higher prices. Unfortunately, the fad stock's price quickly becomes extremely overinflated when compared to the company's true worth.

Many investors lose money in fad stocks because they buy the stock when it is receiving a lot of publicity and the stock price is already high. Eventually, common sense prevails and the stock's price starts to fall (usually after the small investor has just bought it at record high prices). If the investor does not sell quickly, he or she may end up with a stock at a much lower and more reasonable price.

Companies in the high-technology medical industry are prone to fads, especially companies researching cures for major diseases such as cancer or AIDS. Even the rumor that a company may have treatments for such life-threatening diseases can cause a stock to skyrocket. However, the investors who make truly great profits bought when the stock was low, before it became a fad. They didn't follow the crowd that bought the stock at higher and higher prices. Instead, they sold for tremendous profits when everyone else was buying and driving up the price.

Cyclical Stocks

These stocks move up and down in a price cycle. Almost all stocks experience a price cycle to some degree. Blue chips and income stocks may not show a great variation from the low to the high price, while some quality, low-priced stocks may experience huge price swings one or more times a year. Properly analyzing a stock to determine its quality and taking advantage of its price cycles can create high profits for the investor.

Low-Priced Stocks

For my purposes, low-priced stocks refer to stocks costing under $10 per share. There are several kinds of low-priced stocks—from highly speculative penny stocks (stocks selling for less than $1 per share), which I don't recommend, to the other extreme, quality, low-priced stocks (or as I call them, CHEAP stocks). A CHEAP stock is a company with good sales and earnings that is near its 52-week low price. Statistics have proven that quality, low-priced stocks possess great investment potential; thus, this book will concentrate on CHEAP stocks.

COMMON STOCKS OFFER EXCELLENT LIQUIDITY

What is liquidity? Liquidity is the ability to convert assets into cash during a short period of time. This should be a major consideration in any investment that you make. Anyone who has sold a home is familiar with liquidity. In the current slow real estate market, it is not uncommon for months or, in extreme cases, for years to pass between the time a house is offered for sale and actually is sold. While the house price can be determined by professional appraisers, in the end, the house is worth only what someone else is willing to pay for it. Most of the time this is lower than the appraised value.

Investors in collectibles such as coins, stamps, collectors' plates, etc., often find that when they want to sell, the market is small and even though a plate, coin or other collectible may be worth a certain amount according to magazine articles, no one offers anything close to that amount.

During the mid-1980s, a friend of mine decided to invest in the new craze, collectors' plates. He excitedly read about the amazing profits that he could make. One company claimed the distinction of being a collectors' plate exchange and compared itself with a stock exchange. Supposedly, you could buy plates from the company and then when the price went up, you could sell your plate on the exchange. This sounded like a good opportunity.

My friend decided to invest. A Norman Rockwell plate appreciated from my friend's $17 purchase price to a value of $160 according to literature he received from the exchange. He had purchased ten plates so he figured his $170 investment was now worth $1,600 for a 841 percent profit in just two years! When he called the exchange to sell his plates, they confirmed the $160 value but recommended that he discount it by 25 percent so the plate would sell faster. Also, there was a 20 percent commission when the exchange sold his plates. That would net him $96 per plate. This was quite a bit below the $160 value, but still not bad. However, after several months, the plates hadn't sold and when he called the exchange, they suggested he again lower his price. He did—to $75, then $50 and finally $35. In desperation, he visited stores that sold collectors' plates and finally was able to sell six for $192 or $32 each. He never did sell any plates through the exchange. He now keeps one plate hanging above his desk to remind him of that investment. Since then he has invested only in common stocks because he knows that they offer more liquidity and that it will be easier to find a buyer when he wants to sell.

Common stocks that are traded on the NYSE, ASE (American Stock Exchange) or the OTC (Over-the-Counter) National Market System can quickly be bought or sold for specifically quoted prices. You can call your broker, ask for the latest trade price for the stock and then instruct him or her to buy or sell either for a specific price or at the market price (which is the best price available at the time the order is executed).

In most cases, the computerization of the exchanges allows your broker to buy or sell your stock at the market price in a matter of minutes. The great liquidity of common stocks, compared with many other long-term investments, is a tremendous advantage.

Common Stocks Possess Great Profit Potential

Numerous types of investments are available. To mention a few, you can buy gold, real estate, rare coins, diamonds, stamps, silver and other precious metals, rare books, futures, commodities, tax shelters, art and options.

Many investors have tried one or more of these investments with varying degrees of success. In fact, after the 1987 crash, most investors became disillusioned with common stocks for they believed that stocks were too speculative. They decided to put their money in "safer" investments, such as options, commodities or futures.

Because they knew nothing about these investments, some became easy marks for scam artists. Others lost money because they weren't knowledgeable enough to make wise investment decisions. They discovered that the people who really make good profits investing in art, coins, diamonds and other collectibles are experts, educated and specializing in a specific collectible.

I see more and more investors, who turned to other types of investments after the 1987 crash, returning to common stocks poorer but wiser. Over the long term, investments in common stocks have generally grown well ahead of the inflation rate. Since 1947, money invested in common stocks has grown at an average annual rate of better than 11 percent[1], while inflation has averaged under 4.5 percent. In general, common stocks not only have kept up with inflation, but they have produced an additional six-percent profit for the investors.

While a six-percent profit may not seem like much, over the years it can really add up. (See Table 2.1.)

Don't forget these amounts are for growth *above* the inflation rate. This is real purchasing power, which makes quite a difference. Of course, the six-percent growth rate is only an average over a long period of time. Year-to-year fluctuations and poor investment choices can adversely affect that rate. On the other hand, making educated decisions to

---

[1] Standard & Poor's 500 Stock Index.

Table 2.1   Six Percent Growth for $1,000

After	Amount
1 Year	$ 1,060
5 Years	1,338
10 Years	1,791
20 Years	3,207
30 Years	5,743
40 Years	10,286

buy CHEAP stocks with real investment potential can result in a much higher rate of return.

Common stocks are an investment for all times. They represent the *best* investment for the vast majority of individuals. They are attractive because over the long haul, common stocks produce better results than most other investments. They have a ready marketplace for both buying and selling. Common stocks are more appropriate and more affordable for the small investor who may not have much money to invest.

Of course, to make intelligent investment decisions, the investor must be willing to spend some time and effort learning about common stocks. Successful investing in common stocks involves using that knowledge when researching potential investments to determine which is the best for your particular goals. This is time well spent and can reap profitable rewards in the near future.

RISK VERSUS PROFIT POTENTIAL

When you invest, you want to avoid ridiculous risks that will only help you lose money. You also don't want to make an investment without risk for the investment may be so stable that nothing much will happen to it (including increasing in price). You must find a happy medium. One way to reduce your risk factor is to diversify, that is, to invest in more than one stock.

When you contemplate any type of investment, you should consider your risk versus your profit potential. Figure 2.1 shows several types of investments and their risk versus profit potential.

Ironically, the small investor, because he or she does not have much money to invest, must make the best profit possible. A large investor who has $100,000 can afford to invest in U.S. securities, such as treasury

Figure 2.1   Risk Versus Profit Potential

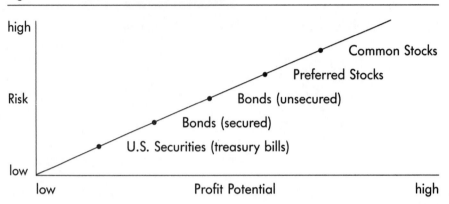

bills at six or seven percent. However, a small investor with only $1,000 or $2,000 in capital needs a higher profit rate or his or her money may never amount to much.

Common stocks offer a high profit potential. However, they also present a greater risk factor. By becoming an educated investor and understanding how the common stock market works, analyzing a stock with good potential, purchasing it at the best price and watching for signs indicating you should take your profit and sell, you can greatly reduce these risks. The majority of the time, if you invest in a high-quality, low-priced stock, your chances of making a profit are excellent.

COMMON STOCKS AND YOUR TAXES

Each time you buy or sell a stock, your brokerage firm will send a confirmation of the trade detailing the price you paid or received for your shares, the number of shares traded and the commission. The brokerage firm also sends a copy of the confirmation to the Internal Revenue Service. *Make sure that you keep all your confirmation forms.* You will need them when you file your taxes.

When listing your stock transactions on tax form Schedule D, remember to subtract your commissions. They are not a part of your profits. Also check with your tax adviser for you should be able to deduct the cost of this book and any financial newsletters and newspapers to which you subscribe.

Capital Gains

Before the 1986 tax revisions, taxpayers could claim both long-term and short-term capital gains. Short-term capital gains were treated as regular income and the percentage of tax owed was determined by the person's income-tax bracket, which could go up to 50 percent. Long-term capital-gains rules applied to stocks held at least six months before they were sold and the highest tax percentage was 20 percent. Unfortunately in 1986, this was changed and all profits were considered taxable income; now the investor pays taxes according to his or her tax bracket. (If you sustain many capital losses, you can offset all your gains and up to $3,000 of taxable income every year until you use up all the losses.)

In 1989 and 1990, President Bush pushed to reduce the long-term capital-gains tax to a 15-percent maximum. Long term in this instance would be defined as being held three years. The Democratic Congress fought against the reduction, claiming it affected only the rich. However, about 60 million Americans would either be directly or indirectly affected for many people are involved in pension funds, profit-sharing and life-insurance plans. If the new tax reduction is ever passed, it would be a boon for our economy as well as for the stock market.

By the way, the United States is the *only* industrial country in the world that even taxes capital gains. Perhaps those foreign investors who buy U.S. stocks have the funds to do so because they don't have to pay capital-gains taxes.

USING YOUR STOCK AS COLLATERAL

An advantage of purchasing stocks instead of other investments is that if an emergency arises, you sometimes can use your stock as collateral for a loan. This creates the opportunity to raise money without selling your stock. This is a great advantage if the stock price happens to be at a low point and you would lose money on your investment if you were forced to sell. This alternative allows you to hold the stock until the price is right for selling.

Banks differ, but normally if your stock is listed in *The Wall Street Journal*, your bank can loan you from 50 percent to as much as 80 percent of the value of the stock. Be aware that as long as the stock price continues to rise, there is no problem. However, if your stock price goes down, for example 30 percent, then your bank probably will require additional collateral.

CHAPTER

$$3$$

How the Stock Exchanges Work

From the visitors' gallery, the floors of the various stock exchanges look like a wild mass of confusion, with people shouting, using strange hand gestures and running back and forth. Believe it or not, that "mass of confusion" is actually very organized and conducts the serious business of buying and selling stocks.

UNDERSTANDING AN EXCHANGE
STOCK TRANSACTION

If an investor wants to buy 1,000 shares of Emerson Radio Corporation at $2.25 per share, she will call her broker, who acts as an intermediary between the client (the buyer) and the seller. For his services, the stock-broker will receive a commission of usually five to ten percent of the stock's cost. The broker takes the order to his office's trading department, which sends his client's order to his brokerage firm's floor broker on the New York Stock Exchange. The floor broker is an employee of the brokerage firm who is a member of the exchange. When the floor broker receives the order for 1,000 shares of Emerson Radio, he will move to the appropriate one out of 22 trading posts on the NYSE floor. There he will join other floor brokers and the specialist who handles Emerson Radio. A typical stock transaction includes the following:

1. An investor wants to buy 1,000 shares of Emerson Radio (EME) at $2.25.
2. The investor calls a stockbroker.
3. The stockbroker takes the order.
4. The stockbroker sends the order to the trading department.
5. The trading department passes on the order to the floor broker.
6. The floor broker buys shares from a specialist.
7. The floor broker confirms the purchase to the trading department.
8. The trading department confirms the order to the broker.
9. The stockbroker confirms the completion of the purchase of 1,000 shares of EME at $2.25 to the client.

At that trading post, Emerson's specialist performs his market-making functions, buying and selling the stock. The floor broker will offer $2.25 for 1,000 shares of Emerson Radio, which will either be accepted or rejected by the specialist. If the offer is accepted, the floor broker purchases the 1,000 shares either from the specialist's own account or from another floor broker who wants to sell 1,000 shares of Emerson Radio through the specialist.

Once he has purchased the stock, the floor broker will send a confirmation of the purchase of 1,000 shares of Emerson Radio at $2.25 per share to his trading department, which, in turn, contacts the broker, who calls his client to advise her of the completion of the purchase. In many cases, with computerization the whole process takes only a few minutes to complete and confirm.

NEW YORK STOCK EXCHANGE (NYSE)

Founded in 1792, the NYSE is the largest stock exchange in the United States. It is located at 11 Wall Street in New York City and is known as the "Big Board" and the "Exchange." Approximately 2,000 of the largest, most well-known and profitable U.S. companies are listed on the NYSE.

The NYSE is an unincorporated association headed by a full-time chairperson and governed by a board of directors representing the public and the exchange membership in about equal proportion. Its functions include membership regulation and surveillance, finance and offices services, product development and planning, market servicing and public relations. The NYSE handles legal problems, government regulations and economic research for member firms.

Affiliated corporations include the Depository Trust Company (DTC), a corporation that acts as a go-between for security transfers. Using the DTC reduces the need for physically transferring certificates and cash by recording entries on its computerized system. The DTC debits and credits each member's account for the net assets changing hands. The National Securities Clearing Committee (NSCC) is a committee formed from the consolidation of clearing operations between the NYSE and the ASE to facilitate the receipt and delivery of security transactions. The Securities Industry Automation Corporation (SIAC) is a subsidiary jointly owned by the NYSE and the ASE to communicate trade information. Besides sharing information between the two exchanges, SIAC provides data to other industry quotation services.

A total of 1,336 seats are on the NYSE that allow the owner to be a member and trade on the floor of the exchange. Most of the seats are owned by brokerage firms. About 550 brokerage firms, including 150 specialists, are responsible for maintaining an orderly market in the securities that they handle. Most members execute orders for the public, for institutions and for mutual funds, while about 25 floor traders deal exclusively for their own accounts. Stocks, bonds, warrants, options and rights are traded on the NYSE.

Listing Requirements for the NYSE

For a company to be listed on the NYSE, it must have:

1. at least one million shares of stock outstanding;
2. a market value of $16 million (Market value equals price per share multiplied by the number of shares outstanding.);
3. at least 2,000 shareholders;
4. a pretax income of $2.5 million average for the past three years or a one-time, pretax income of $6.5 million; and
5. paid a listing fee, which varies depending on the company's size.

Once a company meets with a listing regional manager, it is asked to send specific information to the exchange including its past three years of audited balance sheets, form 10-Ks and annual reports. After reviewing the information, the Listed Company Advisory Committee

(LCAC), which includes chief executive officers (CEOs) and presidents of NYSE member companies, interviews the company. If the LCAC determines that the company meets the requirements, the company is asked to apply formally for listing on the NYSE. Normally, this takes six to ten weeks from the date of application to the company's actual listing on the exchange.

Why go through the hassle to become listed? A major advantage of the NYSE listing is the tremendous exposure a company enjoys after joining the 2,000 elite companies already on the exchange. Interestingly, about 90 percent of major institutional investors only buy stocks that are listed on the NYSE. Another advantage is that it is much easier to raise capital once the company is a member of the NYSE.

The NYSE offers a number of publications of interest to the investor. For further information, contact: Publication Department, New York Stock Exchange, 11 Wall Street, New York, NY 10005, or call (212) 656-2889.

AMERICAN STOCK EXCHANGE (ASE)

The ASE was formed in 1850 around the time of the California gold rush. It is the second most important stock exchange, although it ranks below the National Association of Securities Dealers Automated Quotations (NASDAQ) in terms of volume and dollar value of trading. The ASE was known as the Curb Exchange for almost 70 years because transactions took place on the curb at Trinity Place in New York City and sometimes it is still referred to as the "Curb." In 1921, it moved into its headquarters at 86 Trinity Place. By 1928, it was known as the New York Curb Exchange and not until 1953 was its name changed to the American Stock Exchange.

The ASE operates in a manner similar to the NYSE. It also is an unincorporated association headed by a full-time chairperson and governed by a board of directors. Like the NYSE, the ASE also trades stocks, bonds, warrants, options and rights. In addition, it trades U.S. treasuries. More foreign stocks are traded on the ASE than on any other exchange. Most of the more than 800 stocks listed on the ASE today are small- to medium-sized businesses with a large concentration of oil, gas and mining companies. Many of the larger and well-known companies such as Armour, Borden, Dow Chemical, DuPont, Goodyear, RCA and Standard Oil of California traded on the ASE before moving to the NYSE.

Listing Requirements for the ASE

Companies must meet the following minimum standards to qualify for listing on the ASE. (The membership requirements for the ASE are significantly lower than those for the NYSE.) A company must have:

1. at least 500,000 publicly held shares (exclusive of insider holdings);
2. a tangible net worth of $4 million;
3. a market value of $3 million (price per share multiplied by the number of shares outstanding);
4. a net income of $400,000 for the most recent year;
5. at least 150,000 shares held in lots of 100 to 1,000;
6. a minimum stock price of $5 per share (sometimes waived); and
7. paid a listing fee.

Perhaps the main reason for a stock to move up from the OTC market to the ASE is the increased ease in raising capital. When a stock is listed on the OTC market, it must apply individually to each state in which it wants to sell securities. This is very expensive and time consuming. Once the company is listed on the ASE, it is automatically free to sell its securities in all 50 states.

For more information, contact: American Stock Exchange, 86 Trinity Place, New York, NY 10006, or call (212) 306-1000.

REGIONAL STOCK EXCHANGES

While the term *regional stock exchange* is sometimes used in a derogatory manner, it accurately describes exchange trading located outside of New York. While regional stock exchanges feature listings of a few local companies, the bulk of their business is obtained from national markets. During the 1960s, there were 14 regional exchanges in the United States. Since then, the weak have either merged or expired and only five significant exchanges remain. They are the Midwest, Pacific, Philadelphia, Boston and Cincinnati stock exchanges.

Trading on these exchanges (except for Cincinnati) is pretty much as previously described. Stocks with certain local following may be listed exclusively with that regional exchange, but the majority of the exchange's trading volume is derived from transactions of NYSE-listed stocks. Because of the Intermarket Trading System, it is as easy to buy AT&T from the Boston or Midwest exchanges as it is from the New York

Exchange. Stock-price quotes from the regional specialists are as competitive as, and sometimes better than, the New York quotes.

The Midwest Stock Exchange

This exchange was the result of mergers in 1949 and 1960 of several separate exchanges, including the Chicago, St. Louis, Cleveland, Minneapolis-St. Paul and New Orleans exchanges. Located in the heart of Chicago's financial district, the Midwest is the most active regional exchange by a considerable margin. With 16 exclusive listings, it is obvious that the bulk of trading is in NYSE (and a few ASE) listed companies.

The Pacific Stock Exchange

The Pacific Exchange was formed in 1956 by the merger of the Los Angeles and the San Francisco exchanges. Separate trading floors still are maintained in each city and most of the options trading takes place in San Francisco, while the majority of stock activity is in Los Angeles. The Pacific Exchange offers almost 350 exclusive listings. Interestingly, the Pacific Exchange executes more trades than any other exchange that participates in the Intermarket Trading System except for the NYSE. However, the trades are for smaller volume amounts so the Midwest enjoys a larger market share. The Pacific Exchange does have one big advantage: It is open a half hour later than all the other exchanges.

The Philadelphia Stock Exchange

Founded in 1790 (two years before the NYSE), the Philadelphia Stock Exchange is the oldest organized stock exchange in the United States. During the years, it has merged with the Baltimore and Washington, DC, exchanges. The Philadelphia Exchange has been very successful with options. Perhaps the best known is its foreign-currency option. The options are offered on the Japanese yen, Canadian dollar, Swiss franc, French franc, German mark and British pound. Since 1971, when the value of the U.S. dollar was unlinked with gold, the options have provided valuable hedging tools in the volatile currency markets.

The Boston Stock Exchange

Less than 100 primary listings are on the Boston Exchange and almost all of its trading volume is in NYSE issues. Located so close to New York, it always has had an identity problem and, considering the electronic linking of all the markets, it may have outlived its usefulness. Because Boston is a major location for mutual-funds and money-management firms, the exchange may survive.

The Cincinnati Stock Exchange

The Cincinnati Exchange has been around since 1885 and until 1978 operated as all the other regional exchanges. In May of 1978, Cincinnati began using the Multiple Dealer Trading System, which employs a computer to receive, store and display all orders entered into it. It matches orders to see which can be executed and then completes them. Unlike a specialist, the computerized system makes no market judgments or pricing decisions and executes the orders on a first-come, first-served basis. The system is highly efficient and allows everyone to observe the size and the extent of the orders currently entered. Unfortunately, with the new computer innovations, the "technological advantages" of this system have become somewhat obsolete.

THE OVER-THE-COUNTER MARKET (OTC)

Unlike the NYSE and ASE, which have physical exchange floors, the OTC consists of thousands of securities houses located in hundreds of cities across the country. The securities transactions are handled by a communications network that links the securities houses with each other.

The OTC market lists the largest number of securities— approximately 50,000. The types of securities traded on the OTC market are bank stocks, insurance-company stocks, U.S. government securities, municipal bonds, open-end investment-company shares (mutual funds), railroad-equipment trust certificates, most corporate bonds and tens of thousands of smaller companies' stocks. The OTC market is comprised of securities that, for the most part, do not meet the more demanding listing requirements of the NYSE and the ASE.

The name, Over the Counter, dates back to the late 1700s when Wall Street was enjoying its first bull market and merchants, encouraged by increased activity, kept a small inventory of securities on hand that they sold over the counter along with their other goods.

Virtually all brokerage firms that sell OTC stocks belong to the National Association of Securities Dealers (NASD), which is a nonprofit organization formed under the joint sponsorship of the Investment Bankers Conference and the Securities and Exchange Commission (SEC) to comply with the 1938 Maloney Act.

The basic purpose of the NASD is to standardize OTC trading practices, maintain high moral and ethical standards in securities trading, provide a representative body to consult with the government and investors on matters of importance, establish and enforce fair and equitable rules of securities trading and set up a disciplinary body capable of enforcing these provisions. The NASD also requires that member brokerage firms maintain quick assets (readily convertible assets on hand) in excess of current liabilities at all times.

The OTC market as we know it today began February 5, 1971, with the formation of the NASDAQ, which is owned and operated by the NASD. The NASDAQ is a computerized system that provides brokers and dealers with price quotations for securities traded over the counter. In less than three decades, it has become the second largest market and many times has bettered the NYSE in the total daily share volume.

Any stock wanting to be listed on the NASDAQ system must have:

1. total assets of at least $2 million;
2. capital and surplus of at least $1 million;
3. public float of 100,000 shares;
4. at least 300 shareholders of record and two market makers; and
5. paid a listing fee.

On the NYSE and ASE, the specialists' jobs are to create orderly markets in particular stocks; on the OTC market, the market makers perform the same jobs. Through their computer terminals, market makers enter the highest prices at which they are willing to buy securities and the lowest prices at which they are willing to sell them. This is why OTC stocks show two prices—the bid and the asked.

The *asked price* is the lowest price at which the market maker will sell a stock (i.e., the price the investor pays to buy the stock).

The *bid* is the highest price at which the market maker will buy a stock (i.e., the price the investor will receive if he or she sells the stock).

The *spread* is the difference between the bid and the asked price.

Understanding an OTC Stock Transaction

If an investor wants to buy 100 shares of Tandon, she just calls her broker, who takes the order and sends it to the trading room. If the brokerage firm is a market maker in Tandon, it can execute the order as a principal. If the current bid on Tandon is $1.50 and the asked price is $1.56, the brokerage firm will sell the stock to the investor for $1.56 or perhaps $1.63 but will require no commission. If the brokerage firm is not a market maker, it will buy Tandon from a brokerage firm that is a market maker for the $1.50 price and sell it to the investor at $1.56 plus a commission of up to ten percent of the stock cost. Competition among the various Tandon market makers should guarantee investors the best price available.

The OTC National Market System

In 1982, the OTC devised a new market called the National Market System, which has become the largest traded and most prominent OTC market. It lists more than 3,000 stocks and is published daily in every major newspaper. To be listed in the OTC National Market System, a company must have:

1. a net income of at least $300,000 during the past fiscal year or two out of the past three years;
2. a float of at least 350,000 shares;
3. a market value for the float of $2 million;
4. a minimum bid price of $3 (sometimes waived); and
5. paid a listing fee.

OTC Pink Sheets

If a company does not meet even the minimum NASDAQ requirements, then it becomes listed on the OTC pink sheets, which is a daily publication from the National Quotation Bureau that prints the bid and asked prices and the market makers.

When investing in OTC stocks, make sure that you only invest in stocks that are listed on NASDAQ or on the National Market System for you can easily obtain accurate stock prices. In addition, these companies file quarterly and annual reports with the SEC. In a later chapter, I will discuss the importance of these reports.

I recommend avoiding all pink-sheet stocks because there is no way to accurately follow their stock prices. In many cases, the spread between the bid and the asked price is outrageous. Because these stocks are not required to file any quarterly or annual reports with the SEC, it is virtually impossible to obtain adequate information to make an educated decision on the quality of the stock. While not all pink-sheet stocks are bad investments and a few even become listed on NASDAQ, pink-sheet stocks have been involved in the vast majority of penny-stock scams and violations.

In 1989, the NASD introduced its OTC Bulletin Board, which is an electronic system listing the current bid and asked price of certain pink-sheet stocks. The jury still is out on whether this system will be a success.

Many times, a pink-sheet company will claim that it will shortly be listed on NASDAQ. Occasionally, they do become listed. Many times this is just talk.

STOCK INDEXES AND THEIR MARKET EFFECT

A stock index (or average) measures and reports value changes in representative stock groupings. As an investor, you can compare the movement of your stock to a particular index to see if your investment is performing better or worse than the average. For example, if you own a stock on the NYSE, you may want to compare it to the Dow Jones Industrials, which is probably the premier index.

The Dow Jones Industrial Average (DJIA) is considered the barometer of the stock market. The Dow Jones average was created by Charles H. Dow, the first editor of *The Wall Street Journal*, on July 3, 1884, and consisted of 11 stocks—9 railroad companies and 2 industrial companies.

On March 26, 1896, Dow created his first Dow Jones Industrial Average, which was made up of 12 industrial stocks. In 1928, the average was changed to 30 stocks and even though the companies composing the average have been changed many times, the number has remained at 30. The 30 current Dow Jones Industrial stocks are shown in Figure 3.1.

You may also want to follow the transportation or the utilities averages if you own stocks in these industries. The Dow Jones Transportation Average is an index composed of 20 stocks in the transportation industry, including railway, airline and trucking companies. The Dow

Figure 3.1 Dow Jones Industrials

Alcoa Aluminum Company	Eastman Kodak Co.	J. P. Morgan & Co.
Allied-Signal, Inc.	Exxon Corporation	Philip Morris
American Express Company	General Electric Company	Procter & Gamble Co.
AT&T	General Motors Corporation	Sears, Roebuck & Co.
Bethlehem Steel Corp.	Goodyear Tire & Rubber Co.	Texaco, Inc.
Boeing Company	IBM	Union Carbide Corp.
Caterpillar Inc.	International Paper Co.	United Technologies Corp.
Chevron Corporation	McDonald's Corporation	Walt Disney Co.
Coca-Cola Enterprises, Inc.	Merck & Co., Inc.	Westinghouse Electric Corp.
DuPont	Minnesota Mining & Mfg. Co.	F. W. Woolworth Company

Source: Reprinted by permission of *The Wall Street Journal*, ©1991 Dow Jones & Company, Inc. All Rights Reserved Worldwide.

Jones Utility Average includes 15 stocks in the public-utility industry, such as gas and electric companies.

The New York and American exchanges and the OTC market each have a composite index. The composite indexes express in dollars and cents the change in each market as a whole. The NYSE composite index covers the price movements of all common stocks listed on that exchange. Point changes in the index are converted to dollars and cents to provide a meaningful measure of changes in the average price of listed stocks.

The stocks listed on the Dow Jones Industrials are weighted so that instead of each stock being worth 1/30th of the index, a few stocks have much greater value than the majority of the other stocks. For example, if you look at the Dow Jones Industrials for the first week in January of 1991, you find that IBM is weighted at about 15 percent, Exxon is worth almost 12 percent and General Electric is approximately nine percent. However, Woolworth, Union Carbide and Bethlehem Steel are all weighted under one percent of the total index. I believe that can make the index very misleading. One of the things that has scared the small investor since the 1987 crash has been the tremendous volatility of the Dow Jones Industrials since then. Figure 3.2 delineates the changes in the Dow Jones Industrials for 1990.

If this index indicates either an upward or downward movement, because it is followed by so many analysts, it can influence investors into continuing the trend—which becomes a self-fulfilling prophecy. If everyone believes the market is in trouble and doesn't invest, then the market will be in trouble. I believe that many investors spend too much time worrying about the volatility of the Dow Jones Industrials over the short term. They should be more interested in long-term trends.

Figure 3.2 Dow Jones Industrial Average: 1990

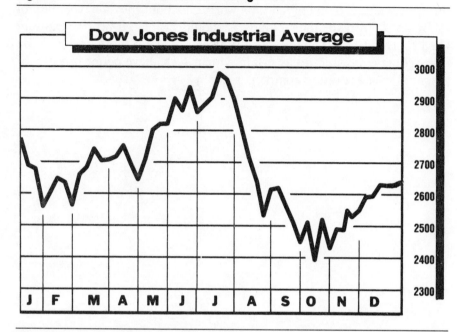

Because all the previously mentioned indexes are composed mainly of higher-priced stocks, they don't adequately reflect the changes occurring in low-priced stocks. Because I was unhappy with those averages, I created my own. The Blue CHEAP Index (BCI) was formed in September of 1981 from 27 NYSE stocks that were under $10 per share at that time. In December of 1987, I revised the BCI and instead of showing dollar changes, I show percent variations that I feel are more accurate. The BCI has consistently outpaced the Dow Jones Industrials by as much as a four-to-one ratio.

I prefer to watch the BCI to get a feel for the low-priced stock market. I also like to follow three indexes that can be found daily in *The Wall Street Journal* and in most major newspapers. The NYSE Advance and Decline Ratio shows the number of stocks up and down on a particular day. The New Highs and Lows is printed both daily and weekly. It lists stocks from all three exchanges and I follow the new lows closely to locate potential turnaround companies. The Biggest Percent Movers indicates both the top percent winners and losers. By following this index, you can discover some of the more volatile cyclical stocks.

The stock indexes should be used as a quick overall guide, but investors shouldn't waste too much time worrying about the daily volatility of the market. Instead, their emphasis should be placed on determining longer-term trends. The investors' time can be spent more profitably by researching companies to ascertain which stocks have better investment potential because of the company's quality.

CHAPTER

$$4$$

Understanding the Investment Process

Buying a stock and watching your money grow is a thrilling idea and it is the basic reason for investing. This nice concept sometimes works and sometimes it doesn't. How did the concept of investing in a company begin in the first place? It started because someone needed money for his or her company and didn't have any other way to raise it. Let's look at the reasons why a company decides to offer part of its ownership to the public.

WHY A COMPANY DECIDES TO SELL STOCK

While most companies are started with capital from the founder or his or her family or friends, there almost always comes a time when more capital is needed. Perhaps it is necessary to research a new idea for a product or to develop the product so it can be marketed. The company may want to expand its marketing areas or consolidate or modernize various production and corporate offices into a larger, more efficient facility. Whatever the reason, the company must obtain additional capital to execute the change. Many times banks are hesitant to lend money to a company when it needs capital (a catch-22 situation), so the company's only alternative may be to sell shares of stock to the public. Buying stock gives the investor the opportunity to purchase part of the ownership of the company and grants the investor the right to some voice in how the company is run.

Before the company makes the decision to offer stock, it must consider the advantages and disadvantages of going public. The advantages include the following:

- The main advantage is obtaining needed capital.
- The capital can be used in many beneficial ways, including increasing working capital, expanding research and development, extending the company's market, hiring additional employees, updating or expanding facilities, retiring existing debt, providing capital for acquisitions or increasing the company's net worth.
- The shares can be used to attract key-management or technical people or to motivate the current work force through stock-option or profit-sharing programs.
- Through the public offering, the company gains prestige with more than 100,000 brokers nationwide, increases its visibility through public-relations press releases sent to national media and enhances its relationship with its bankers.
- A public offering also assigns a value to the company in case it is entertaining the idea of merging or being acquired. It designates a price for the private shares held by the original owners and management.
- Public shares can be used as collateral and borrowed against or sold when additional monies are needed in the future.
- A public offering will expand the company's borrowing capability and allow it to obtain favorable credit terms for future borrowing.
- For the founders of the company, a public offering provides the fulfillment, usually after many years of hard work, of wealth, power and prestige.

The disadvantages of going public include the following:

- Going public involves a relatively high expenditure of capital (from $25,000 to $300,000 depending on the size of the offering) with no certain guarantee that enough investors will want to buy the stock to make it valuable.
- The company will lose privacy. It must make public information about its sales, profits, losses, mode of operation, competitive position, managements' salaries, lawsuits and many other aspects affecting the company.
- Additional costs will be involved to keep the shareholders up to date with annual reports, quarterly reports, press releases, etc. After

going public, most companies are required to file quarterly and annual reports (10-Q and 10-K) with the SEC. Legal costs usually skyrocket because of the need for additional legal expertise to write the regulatory reports. Typical expenses for reports and legal fees can cost as much as $100,000 or more a year.

- The company's management loses some of its decision-making control to the shareholders for major decisions such as conducting a merger or changing its name.
- More pressure is exerted on the company to show increased sales and earnings each year.

This is an important decision for a company to make. In many cases, if the company wants to continue to grow, going public may be the only logical choice. This works to the advantage of investors for it gives investors the opportunity to invest in some great companies.

SPECIALIZING IN ONE AREA
RATHER THAN IN MANY

One of the biggest mistakes an investor can make is spending too much time looking at too many different types of investments. The investor ends up spreading herself too thin and learns a little about a lot and not a lot about anything. The average investor has just so much time that she can devote to developing an understanding of investments. To be a more efficient investor, I believe that your time is better spent specializing in a particular type of investment that interests you.

☐   RULE 3   ☐

Don't be a jack-of-all-trades and a master of none—
specialize in one specific area.

Once you start to learn about a certain type of investment, you begin to realize just how much you don't know and this can be overwhelming. There is much to assimilate, such as how the investment works, why it goes up and down in value, how to research that investment, what criteria point to a more potentially successful investment and what is the best way to make money in that investment. It takes a long time to master just one area of investments. I learned that years ago and devoted my time to stocks under $10 per share. I believe this specialization in an area I understand has been a major contribution to the success of *The CHEAP Investor* newsletter.

There are many different ways to specialize: You can restrict your investigations to a certain type of investment, such as common stocks, options, futures or mutual funds. This book is limited to common stocks with a small section on warrants. However, there are perhaps 60,000 common stocks listed on the NYSE, ASE, OTC, pink sheets and foreign exchanges. I decided to focus on stocks under $10 listed on the NYSE, ASE and OTC NASDAQ, which reduced the number to about 9,000 stocks. Then I specialized further by looking only at quality stocks (profitable, established companies), which further decreased the base to approximately 3,000 stocks, a more manageable number.

If that is still too many stocks for you, you may want to restrict your research to certain industries, specific prices or particular exchanges. Doing that will reduce the amount of companies to a number that you can comfortably investigate. Spending your time researching various companies in the area in which you specialize can be extremely profitable. Focusing your attention on a much smaller area may allow you to surprise your friends and yourself with the competent opinions you are able to voice on those stocks. (Your opinion, if well researched, may be more knowledgeable than that of many "experts.")

THE GREED/FEAR TRAP

During the bull markets of the 1980s, we witnessed some tremendous increases in stock prices. Many investors saw their stocks move up quickly and continued to watch as the prices fell back to or below their original purchase prices. Those investors showed fantastic paper profits, but they didn't take them. When the stock prices started to fall, the investors figured the prices would rise again. Instead the investors' paper profits disappeared and they lost their opportunities to make nice profits.

☐   **RULE 4**   ☐

Don't fall victim to the greed/fear trap.

What happened? I call it the greed/fear trap. Figure 4.1 illustrates this problem. The investor buys a quality, low-priced stock at $1 per

Figure 4.1   Greed/Fear Trap

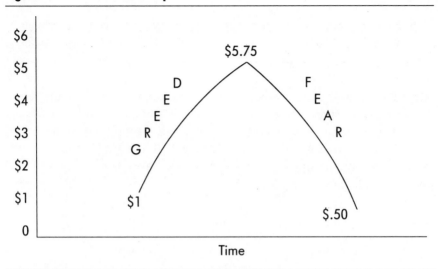

share. The stock price starts to rise, hitting $2, $3, $4, $5, up to a high of $5.75. The investor now has a tremendous profit and decides to sell when the stock hits $6.

The investor has held the stock because of greed. With every upward movement in the stock price, he congratulates himself and figures out how much money he has made. Perhaps the stock moved up fast and he says to himself, "Gee, if it has moved up this much in only two months, imagine how high it will be after four months!"

This kind of greed in itself is not wrong. After all, why would anyone want to invest in a stock except for the greedy reason of making money? However, if greed keeps the investor from realizing a profit, it becomes a liability. The final mistake the investor makes is letting this greed cause him or her to enter a sell order at $6. The investor wants to make a few more cents profit per share. It doesn't matter that the stock has already made a fantastic profit, moving from $1 to $5.75 or +475 percent. If Murphy's Law (anything that can go wrong will go wrong) is operating, the stock will never reach $6 before falling.

Greed has kept the investor from taking a profit because he or she is sure that the stock will continue to rise. Normally, when a stock moves up fast, it falls even faster. Once the stock starts to fall, the investor rationalizes that, "I can't sell it at $5 because it was at $5.75 only yesterday and I'm sure it will go back up." Then as the stock continues to fall, the investor becomes afraid to take the profit and reasons that, "I can't sell the stock for only $3 when it was $5.75. It will go up again and I'll miss

Table 4.1 Stop-Loss Prices

STOCK PRICE	$2.00	$3.00	$4.00	$5.00	$6.00	$7.00	$8.00	$9.00	$10.00
STOP LOSS	1.63	2.13	3.13	4.13	4.88	5.88	6.88	7.88	8.88

out if I sell now." This continues until the stock usually ends up below the original purchase price, perhaps at $ .50. Then the unhappy investor just wishes the stock would go back up to the original $1 purchase price so he or she can break even. (I'm sure that anyone who has ever invested can at one time or another recognize himself or herself as a victim of the greed/fear trap.)

PROTECTING YOURSELF FROM THE GREED/FEAR TRAP

The smart investor recognizes how easy it is to fall into the greed/fear trap and learns to avoid it. He can protect himself with a stop-loss order. As the stock price moves up, he raises the stop loss; but if the price experiences a serious drop, the stock will automatically be sold and he will realize a profit.

For example, if you bought a stock at $1 and it moved up to $2, you could call your broker and enter a stop-loss order for $1.63. The stop loss should automatically sell your stock if it drops to $1.63. You have made a nice profit and have protected yourself in case the stock price drops further. As the stock price continues to move upward, your stop loss should be adjusted. Table 4.1 shows suggested stop-loss prices.

Notice that the suggested stop loss for $2 is $1.63. Why not $1.75? Because that is where most investors would put it. To avoid a problem with selling your stock because too many other orders have also been entered, refrain from setting stop losses on the even dollar, $ .50 or $ .25 amounts. At the $2, $3 and $4 prices, the stop loss is $ .87 below the price; however, at the $6 through $10 level, it is $1.12 less. Why? Because the higher the stock price moves, the more volatility the stock has.

You want to protect your profit, yet you also don't want the stock sold just because the price jumped around a little. At higher prices, the major resistance point is usually at the dollar level. Therefore if your stock hits $9, it may back off to $8 before continuing upward. If your stop loss had been set at $8.13, the stock would have been sold and while you would have made a nice profit, there was potential for more. As you can see, it is a delicate job to set the stop loss high enough to keep your profit, but not so high that the stock gets sold when the price backs off somewhat.

If your stock moves up nicely and you enjoy a 50-percent profit in a couple of months, you are never "wrong" to take a profit on a stock. Granted the stock may continue upward and you could have made even more profit; however, too many of us get caught up by greed, holding on for just a little more and ending up right back where we started (or even worse). Don't let yourself get caught. Protect your profits. Take them when you think it is wise and don't look back and berate yourself because you could have made more. That just wastes time and energy. You'll be busy enough analyzing potential investments and checking on the ones you have already made.

CHAPTER

5

Analyzing Stocks
Easily and Profitably

An investor's ultimate goal is to discern which investment affords the greatest profit potential. Some people let their brokers decide for them. Others pick a name that sounds familiar and has the ring of quality. A few have even tried the dart-board method of choosing stocks. (The investor throws a dart at a listing of stocks and buys the one that is hit.)

Choosing an investment is easy. However, if the investor wants to actually determine if the stock is a good investment, then he or she must analyze it. Making the effort to carefully check out an investment before buying it positions an individual in a select category of investors—the smart ones.

FUNDAMENTAL AND TECHNICAL ANALYSIS

While many variations exist, there are two major ways to analyze stocks. Fundamental analysis covers the study of all relevant financial information about the company that can influence the future course of its stock price. Technical analysis is the examination of all factors related to the actual supply and demand for the company's stock.

Fundamental Analysis

This type of stock analysis evaluates the worthiness of a security by examining the company's tangible assets and financial strength. It focuses on elements such as book value, earnings per share and price-earnings ratio, along with the stock's price in relation to its 52-week high-low range. Fundamental analysis considers past records of assets, earnings, sales, products, management and markets when predicting future trends in the company's success or failure. Fundamental analysts may consider outside factors that could influence the company, such as the economic situation, government policy and the company's stature within its industry. The primary source of the data used in the analysis is the company's own financial statements, which can be found in its annual, 10-K, 10-Q and quarterly reports.

Fundamental analysis received much publicity, which created a great following during the 1930s depression when stocks were selling at perhaps 10 to 20 percent of their real value. *Security Analysis and Techniques* by Benjamin Graham and David Dodd, which was first printed in 1934, is the bible of fundamental analysis. In the book's preface, the authors wrote of their decision to place "much emphasis. . . upon distinguishing the investment from the speculative approach, upon setting up sound and workable tests of safety and upon an understanding of the rights and true interests of investors in senior securities and owners of common stock." Investors wanted to read that during the 1930s and I believe the same holds true today.

The premise of fundamental analysis is to examine a company's financial statement and other relevant information to discover if it is selling significantly below its worth. If so, the investor purchases the stock and waits until the rest of the world recognizes the stock's value. Sooner or later, the stock price should move up closer to its true value. When the stock price goes up because everyone wants to buy the stock, that is the time to sell and to use fundamental analysis to locate another undervalued company.

T. Boone Pickens uses fundamental analysis to locate potential takeover candidates. Evaluating the fundamentals of a company allows Pickens to determine if the break-up value is greater than the stock price. (The break-up value is what the stock could be worth if all the assets of the company were sold.) Pickens has used this type of analysis very successfully to identify profitable take-over candidates.

Technical Analysis

Usually, technical analysis thrives during times of economic prosperity or during bullish periods when stock prices are rising and trading profits are easy to make. In such times, many analysts may revise their view of fundamental analysis and consider it out of date.

Technical analysts (or technicians) study all the factors related to the supply and demand of stocks. Through the use of stock charts, technicians seek various indicators that herald the change in the price or the volume of a particular stock. The major advantage of using technical analysis is that it shows a picture of the stock's price history. The simplest type of a chart is a bar chart that indicates the high price, low price and closing price for the time period that can be calculated on a daily, weekly, monthly or yearly basis. Figure 5.1 is a bar chart that shows a week's worth of high, low and closing prices.

A volume chart for a week may look like Figure 5.2.

In technical analysis, the investor is looking for patterns that could indicate which way the stock price will move. Figure 5.3 shows four basic patterns used in this type of analysis.

Technicians believe that because people make markets and people don't change that much, under similar conditions they will repeat their previous actions. Therefore, technical analysis involves the study of statistics for certain transactions to determine the direction of a stock's or market's future price. The technicians have concluded that those stocks or markets contain enough predictable elements to assure the profitability of such studies over a period of time.

While a technician's charts are easy to read, using them correctly is more difficult. The analyst must anticipate where the stock is going and

Figure 5.1   Price Chart

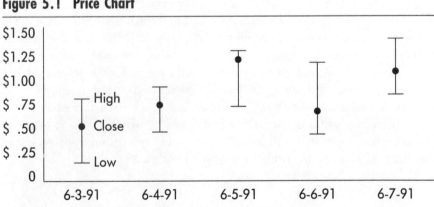

Figure 5.2   Volume Chart

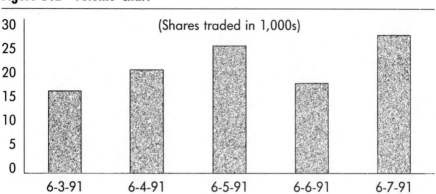

the chart can be misleading, especially if it just shows a short period of time. Charting a stock for a period of months or years may show cyclical trends that occur around the same time each year. For example, a stock's price may rise shortly before it announces its quarterly dividend and then may fall rapidly thereafter. Determining such a pattern can give the investor an added profit-making edge.

Technicians study the market using various indicators, including the evaluation of the economic variables within a market. Many stocks move with the market because they react to various demand-and-supply forces. That is, if investors want to buy more stock than is available, the price will go up. If more stock is being sold than there are buyers for it, the price will go down. Technical analysis can work well with stocks that

Figure 5.3   Basic Patterns in Technical Analysis

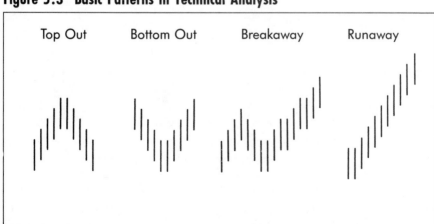

tend to follow the market in general, such as the Dow Jones index stocks and other blue chips. However, I have found that this type of analysis doesn't work well with lower-priced stocks because bargain stocks don't consistently follow the market.

Some technicians follow the trading volume for they believe that it can indicate whether or not a stock or a market is healthy. Presumably, the stock or market price will follow the volume trend. However, I have found that this is not always true.

An interesting variation of technical analysis is the Odd-Lot Theory that is based on contrary opinion. The theory concludes that historically, the odd-lot traders (small investors who trade in less than 100-share quantities) are usually guilty of bad timing. When odd-lot volume rises in an up stock market, the odd-lot analyst views it as a sign of technical weakness that signals a market reversal. Basically, the technician determines what the odd-lot traders are doing and does the opposite.

You may have heard of a third theory for investment called Random Walk. This philosophy of investment discounts both fundamental and technical analysis. It concludes that at least in the short run, the market pricing is completely at random, that there is no pattern for every price movement is independent of the previous one—so much for technical analysis. It also assumes that the market is efficient so there are no underpriced or overpriced stocks and that dismisses fundamental analysis. What is left? Well, there is always the dart board to pick your stocks. However, my best success has come from using fundamental analysis.

Comparing Fundamental and Technical Analysis

Let's look at fundamental and technical analysis in action. In November of 1990, I recommended AST Research, an OTC National Market System stock selling at $15. Why? Because I believed AST was strong in the fundamentals, including its balance sheet, which showed that the company had increased its year-end sales from $456 million to $533 million. AST's net income jumped from a loss of $7.5 million in 1989 to a profit of $35.1 million in 1990, yet its stock was selling near its 52-week low. In addition, the company had reduced its long-term debt from $81 million to $30 million, while its cash assets increased from $18 million to $92.3 million.

Despite the turnaround in its balance sheet, I believed the stock's price was exceedingly low. A technician looking at AST would not have been impressed with it because there was no upward trend to indicate that the stock's price would continue to rise. About eight weeks after I had recommended the stock at $15, the trading volume increased as it rose to $38 or 153 percent. Because the stock price and volume were now showing an upward trend, a technician may have been interested in AST at $38, but that is more than 150 percent higher than what my subscribers paid for it.

AST has experienced several price swings. In February of 1988, I recommended it at $8.38 and it rose to $17.38 or + 107 percent. In September of 1988, I again advised purchasing the stock at $9 and it rose to $26.13 or + 190 percent! Both times, my fundamental analysis indicated that AST was a bargain stock, yet technical analysis of the company's volume would not have indicated that it was worth purchasing until it was much higher in price.

I believe AST is a prime example of the benefits of using fundamental analysis to discover a quality investment. In many cases, fundamental analysis allows the investor to buy a stock at a much lower price instead of waiting until the stock's price and volume increase dramatically on technical charts to indicate that it is a good buy. That is the main reason I use fundamental analysis and perhaps why *The CHEAP Investor* has recommended so many stocks before the Wall Street analysts become interested in them.

LEARNING FROM ANNUAL, 10-K, 10-Q AND QUARTERLY REPORTS AND PRESS RELEASES

To analyze a stock, you need several publications that can be obtained directly from the company. You can either call or write the company to request its annual report, the 10-K and 10-Q reports, its latest quarterly report and any press releases. The information contained in these reports can help you determine whether or not a stock is a potentially profitable investment.

Annual Report

The formal yearly report of a corporation's financial condition that the SEC requires to be distributed to shareholders is the annual report. In addition to financial reports and notes from an independent certified public accountant, the report commonly contains a summary of the products or services, a progress report, comments from the president and chairperson on the company's financial and industry status and reports on corporate expansion and new products.

Most annual reports are designed by the company's advertising or public-relations department to promote the company to the reader. The report, which generally should be written in easy-to-understand language, explains the company's products and goals. The report can be very basic, printed in black and white, or it can run the gamut to include multiple colors on glossy paper with attractive pictures to impress the shareholder. A company with poor financial results may invest in an extremely expensive-looking annual report, hoping that it will give the impression that the company is a good investment. Don't be fooled.

Financial Statement

While annual reports vary greatly, they all contain financial statements that are audited, written records of the company's financial status. The financial statement consists of five parts: the consolidated balance sheet, the income statement, the statement of changes in financial position, the statement of retained earnings and notes to the financial statements.

Consolidated Balance Sheet   A company's balance sheet presents its financial position in detail. It shows the balance of its various types of assets, liabilities and shareholder equity as of a specific date (usually the end of the month). The assets are basically what the company owns, the liabilities are what it owes and the shareholder's equity is the value of the stock after all the liabilities are subtracted from the assets.

Income Statement   This report provides information concerning the total revenues, costs, expenses and net earnings from operations.

Statement of Changes in Financial Position   An audited report, it presents information concerning the company's operating, financing and investing activities. The statement indicates any changes in the company's financial position during the year.

Statement of Retained Earnings   This is a combined statement of the company's yearly income and retained earnings. Retained earnings is the total amount of cumulative net profits reinvested in the corporation after the payment of dividends.

Notes to the Financial Statements   This final report provides an explanation of specific items in the financial statement. The notes are extremely important for they may contain positive or negative information that could have a significant impact on the company. As a potential investor, you will want to read them carefully.

What To Look For in the Annual Report

There is no standardized form for annual reports so I can only generalize. On the inside of the annual report's front cover is usually a corporate profile detailing the company's main areas of business. If the company's earnings are very positive, the report will probably contain a section on selected financial data comparing three to five years of sales (or revenues), net income, net income per share and the number of shares outstanding. Have the sales and net income improved compared to the previous year or years?

Many annual reports contain a financial-highlights section that details sales, earnings, assets, liabilities and shareholder's equity. Look for increases in the assets and in the shareholder's equity and decreases in the liabilities. Read the notes below the financial data to see if there is anything extremely positive or negative.

The letter to the shareholders is written by the chairperson of the board and/or the president. It details what has happened to the company during the past year and presents the goals that the company hopes to accomplish during the next year. Typically, the letter is extremely positive, looking on the bright side, regardless of the company's performance during the past year.

If you like what you have seen so far, find the section in the Financial Statement called the Notes to the Financial Statement and read them carefully. Toward the end of the annual report should be a section on litigation. It is not unusual for lawsuits to be brought against a company; however, you should investigate to see if the company has insurance to cover the cost if it loses any lawsuit. If the company is suing another company or individual for a large amount of money, this could prove extremely positive if the company wins. (In fact, MCI received a big boost by suing AT&T and winning.)

Look at the accountant's letter. Many times, reading the letter will give you some insight, especially the paragraph starting with "In our opinion. . . ." Is the company's accountant a major company? If so, that is positive.

The number of shareholders can also be important and a stock with at least 1,000 shareholders is best. A large number of shareholders indicates that there are many small shareholders. When selling occurs in a stock with only a small number of shareholders, it can cause the stock to be more volatile especially on the downside.

The market-information section indicates which exchange the stock is traded on and its symbol and gives two years (by quarters) of its high and low prices. The example below shows that there may be quite a variation between the high and the low price depending on the quarter.

	Bid Prices	
Year-End December 31, 1990	High	Low
Fourth Quarter	$6.50	$3.13
Third Quarter	3.50	2.75
Second Quarter	5.38	2.25
First Quarter	3.88	3.75

	Bid Prices	
Year-End December 31, 1989	High	Low
Fourth Quarter	$5.00	$2.75
Third Quarter	4.25	3.50
Second Quarter	5.00	2.13
First Quarter	3.00	2.38

It is not uncommon for a stock to trade at higher prices during certain quarters. In the above example, a stock has traded for a higher price in the second and fourth quarters. If you check the company's sales and earnings for these quarters, you may find a correlation between the sales and earnings and the stock price. Many companies experience seasonal sales and those quarters may be historically better than others.

Form 10-K

This report is filed with the SEC by all companies with at least 500 shareholders and $1 million or more in assets (basically all NYSE, ASE and OTC NASDAQ listed companies). The SEC requires that certain information must be listed in the 10-K and that it must be filed within 90 days after the close of the fiscal year. Because the 10-K is written by the financial department and sent to the SEC, it gives more explicit information about the company and its divisions, finances and products than the annual report does.

The 10-K may seem complicated at first, but it becomes easier to read with practice. It includes information about the company: its industry; competitors; regulations; patents and trademarks; accessibility of raw materials; locations of each division, office, franchise, etc.; order backlog; research and development; environmental regulations; employees; foreign and domestic operations; export sales; description of properties, including location, size, cost and lease-expiration date; marketing; employment agreements; full information on all legal proceedings; company stock-market information; complete annual financial statements; liquidity and capital resources; management's description and analysis of the financial condition and results of operations; inflation and price changes; expenses—why they changed and specific factors that caused the change; information and background on the directors and the executive officers; executive compensation, including bonuses; profit-sharing, bonus and retirement plans; employee stock ownership, including the number of shares owned and the price paid by all officers and directors; and information on various types of securities offered by the company.

While all this information is interesting, some is more important to the stock price than others. If you don't have the annual report, then check the 10-K's financial statements, looking for improvements. Read through the litigation to determine if there are any lawsuits that could either be very positive or negative for the company. Look at the stock-market information to see if the price has any cyclical tendencies.

I would suggest that you check the management's compensation. Is it out of line with the company's finances? (Many companies have been bled dry by outlandish management salaries and stock-option or bonus programs.) The 10-K will contain the pertinent information if a Form 8-K has recently been filed with the SEC. A Form 8-K is required by the SEC following any event that affects the company's financial situation.

Learn if any warrants are outstanding. If so, what is the exercise price and the expiration date? Does the company plan a public or private offering of stock? In either case, this could affect the price of the stock for there will be more shares outstanding to dilute the value of the stock once the offering is completed or the warrant is exercised.

Always check the company's cash situation. If the cash situation is extremely low or the company is in a deficit position, the company may have to raise capital in the near future with a public or private offering that could severely weaken the current share's value.

Form 10-Q

This report is filed with the SEC 45 days after the end of the quarter. It is similar to the 10-K but much smaller. It will, of course, present the latest quarterly financial results. It is important to check these numbers for positive or negative changes that should be taken into consideration when analyzing the company's investment potential.

The 10-Q contains the management's analysis of the quarter, any 8-K filings and the notes to the financial statement. All these should be examined. Basically, you are looking for any changes in the company's overall picture.

Quarterly Report

Usually one folded page, the quarterly report is sent to the shareholders to describe the current financial condition of the company. It contains the sales, net income, net income per share, number of shares outstanding and sometimes the shareholder's equity and compares it with the previous year's quarter. Analyze the figures for improvements. A short letter to the shareholders may be included. It may comment on the quarterly figures and tell about any new developments during the past three months.

Press Releases

If the company also sent press releases or product information, you can read these to help you analyze the company.

GETTING THE FACTS BEFORE YOU INVEST

One of the main reasons people lose money is that they invest on the word of a relative, friend or broker. Many times the information is completely wrong because each time it was passed from one person to another, something was added or deleted. If it was passed through enough people, the original information has probably been totally distorted. Even brokers experience problems, for many times they don't analyze a stock themselves but rely on their brokerage firm's analysts. This is fine except that the analysts may not have the time to update their information as often as they should so the information the broker gets may be obsolete.

If you have an annual report, a 10-K, a 10-Q, a quarterly report and press releases, you probably have as much or more information than most stockbrokers and analysts have. Using that information wisely can make the difference between making or losing money. By doing your research first, you will know that the information is accurate and that you have increased your odds for a profit.

FINDING THE NEXT SUPERSTOCK

Taking the time to obtain the various company reports, read them carefully and analyze the stock's strong and weak points to see if it is a good buy, can be well worth the effort. This is what I do and it has proven to be quite a successful method.

My ultimate goal when researching a company's stock is to find one with perfect criteria. The company must provide superior products or services. Its management team must possess the expertise to efficiently market that product or service, strive to improve sales and earnings, continue expansion with new products or services and search for new markets to penetrate. If the company's stock is at a good low price, then it fulfills the qualifications for the next potential superstock.

Three key items that can almost guarantee a stock-price jump include:

1. The company is producing record sales.
2. The company is achieving record earnings.
3. The company's stock price is near its 52-week low.

Several of my big stock winners fit these criteria when I researched them. A few are shown here:

Company Name	Recommended Price	High Since Recommendation
Envirodyne Industries	$2.81	$80.00 (buyout)
Grolier, Inc.	1.81	27.50 (buyout)
Radice Corporation	2.88	18.25

My statistics indicate that if you find a stock that satisfies the previously mentioned three criteria, your chances of the stock moving upward are more than 90 percent. If the company continues to achieve record sales and earnings, the chances are excellent that the stock price will soar. The great advantage of this approach is that you buy a stock way before the Wall Street analysts are interested. In fact, by the time they become interested in it (because it has moved up so high), it will be time for you to think about taking your profit. If you follow my lead and carefully analyze the fundamentals of any stock you are considering for an investment, perhaps you, too, can find the next superstock and reap a tremendous profit.

CHAPTER

6

Mastering Stocks under $10

Since 1976, I have taught about investing in quality, low-priced stocks or as I call them, CHEAP stocks. Obviously, the small investor with a limited amount of capital needs a higher percent of return than an investor with a large amount of investment capital. For example, if a small investor with only $3,000 and a large investor with $100,000 invest in a security with a guaranteed annual return of ten percent, the small investor only receives $300 while the large investor collects $10,000.

$$\$100,000 \times 10 \text{ percent} = \$10,000$$
$$3,000 \times 10 \text{ percent} = \$300$$

Because the smaller investor is starting with a more modest amount of capital, he or she needs a higher rate of return (30, 40 or 50 percent) to help that capital grow. I have spent years researching different-priced stocks to find which may be more advantageous for the small investor. Through the practical application of various investment theories, I have concluded that CHEAP stocks offer a far greater growth potential, which the small investor needs. The higher-priced, blue-chip stocks have, for the most part, already experienced their major growth cycle and thus do not provide a high enough rate of return. In fact, many of those stocks tend to be overpriced and their prices probably will move down.

☐   RULE 5   ☐

Don't lose money by investing in the wrong price stocks.

When investors buy higher-priced stocks, they encounter two obstacles to success. The first is they can't afford to buy as many shares and the commission fees can eliminate a good portion of their profit. The second obstacle is that many higher-priced stocks are so expensive that it is virtually impossible for the stocks to double in price. The CHEAP stocks offer a much greater growth potential than the long-established, high-priced stocks.

TREMENDOUS POTENTIAL VERSUS BLUE CHIPS

Again and again, I have seen quality, low-priced stocks far outpace the blue chips and I believe that it is much easier for a company such as Tandon Corporation to move from $ .75 to $1.50 than for IBM to double from $100 to $200. I discovered that people who made fortunes owning today's blue-chip stocks bought them years ago when the stocks were much cheaper and the investors could buy many more shares.

The small investor who has only $3,000 to invest must have his or her money work hard. While it may be tempting to buy blue-chip stocks because they are "safer," they are so expensive that $3,000 will not buy many shares.

☐   RULE 6   ☐

To make profits, carefully consider the number of shares you control.

For example, you have $3,000 to invest. You can either buy Tandon at $ .75 or IBM at $100. As you can see, you would be able to purchase 4,000 shares of Tandon and only 30 shares of IBM.

$3,000 ÷ by $ .75 per share for Tandon = 4,000 shares
$3,000 ÷ by $100 per share for IBM = 30 shares

If both stocks rose $1, your profit is much greater with Tandon than with IBM because you are able to buy more shares. As you can see, the more shares you own, the higher your profit.

$$4,000 \text{ shares of Tandon} \times \$1 = \$4,000$$
$$30 \text{ shares of IBM} \times \$1 = \$30$$

Although the Wall Street media report stock movements in points, I believe that when comparing blue-chip stocks to stocks under $10, it is important to figure your profits in percentages rather than in points. Think about it; when it comes to financial matters, almost everyone uses percentages. The IRS taxes your income by a variable percent, your bank lends money to buy a new home or car and charges a certain percent interest, even your credit-card company expects you to pay a percentage finance charge. Doesn't it make sense to look at your investment profits in percentages, too?

It is easy to be impressed by a stock that has jumped a couple of points in one day. Because blue-chip stocks cost so much, the actual profit may not be so great as it seems. Wall Street gets excited when IBM moves up five points to $105 and the jump will be reported on almost all the business news programs. However, a $1 stock that jumps up $ .25 is usually forgotten. In fact, IBM only moved up five percent while the $1 stock rose 25 percent! Which would you rather have owned?

☐   RULE 7   ☐

Always look at profits and losses in percentages, not in points.

In the previous example, if Tandon increased by only $ .25 and IBM jumped up $15, offhand, it would look like IBM had performed better. If you figure out the profit percentages, you would see a different story, for Tandon's $ .25 increase is a 33 percent profit and IBM's huge $15 increase is a mere 15 percent profit.

$$4,000 \text{ Tandon shares} \times \$ .25 \text{ increase} = \$1,000 \text{ profit}$$
$$\$1,000 \text{ profit} \div \text{ by } \$3,000 \text{ purchase price} = 33 \text{ percent}$$

$$30 \text{ IBM shares} \times \$15 \text{ increase} = \$450 \text{ profit}$$
$$\$450 \text{ profit} \div \text{ by } \$3,000 \text{ purchase price} = 15 \text{ percent}$$

Of course, because you are comparing the same amount of invest-ment ($3,000), it is pretty easy to see which stock gave you the greater profit. However, it would be rare that you would invest the same amount of money in all your stocks. Therefore, looking at the percent of profit is the only accurate way to compare just how well your investments have done.

These examples illustrate three important points:

1. Many people lose money in the stock market because they invest in the wrong price stocks. Typically, you can make more money with a quality $ .75 stock than with a blue-chip $100 stock and the growth potential is far greater with the growing $ .75 stock than with the mature $100 stock.
2. An important key to making money in the stock market is the num-ber of shares you control. A $3,000 investment can control 4,000 shares of a $ .75 stock and only 30 shares of a $100 stock.
3. Always look at profits and losses in percentages, not points. If you had just looked at how many points Tandon and IBM had risen, you would have been tempted to say that IBM had done quite a bit better than Tandon. In reality, Tandon was a more profitable invest-ment.

LOCATING A CHEAP INVESTMENT

Finding the companies to research as potential investments involves ac-tively searching for them. You should look at the companies in the area where you live. It is extremely easy to get information and see how well a company's product is doing when it is located nearby. You can just call or stop into its business offices and request information. A few years ago, I became aware of a NYSE-listed company that was just five miles from my office. It fit my investing criteria so I put it on the Blue CHEAP In-dex. Jepson Corporation moved from $5.57 on December 11, 1987, to a high of $13.13 in about six months.

Always be on the lookout for new companies when you are dining out, traveling or just socializing. If you are impressed by a company's new product or service, chances are good that many others will be too. Several years ago, while on a trip to San Francisco, I saw a unique res-taurant surrounded by real railroad cars. Customers could sit in the cars while eating or drinking. The restaurant was extremely busy and as I talked with other people in line, they said it was always that way. My in-terest was piqued. After a good dinner, I asked the manager if the restaurant, Victoria Station, was public. He said it was and the stock was selling for around $2.50. Over the next couple of years, Victoria Station rose to more than $20!

A good source for potential investments is the business section in your local newspaper. You should also start to at least glance through *The Wall Street Journal, Investor's Daily* and *Barron's*. (All three newspapers should be available in your local library.)

Another way to find potential investments is to subscribe to a stock newsletter. Newsletters can be a great source of investments; however, you will want to research before you buy. Avoid newsletters that offer only one buy recommendation. If the newsletter has a good following, recommending only one stock will almost ensure that the stock will soar in price. However, the stock may move up too quickly for the average investor to buy at the low price. Make sure the newsletter lists a specific buy price and gives the name, address and telephone number of the company so you can contact it for further information. If the newsletter gives only a broker's name and telephone number, be careful that he or she doesn't push you into buying something you really don't want.

Listing Stocks for Further Research

A good place to find and research bargain stocks is your main library. Using a copy of *The Wall Street Journal* or *Barron's*, go through the NYSE stocks and make a list of all profitable companies under $10 near their 52-week low price. I use the form in Figure 6.1 to gather all the pertinent information. (When you hear of an interesting company, add it to this checklist.)

Once you have made the list of potential investments, then you can refer to other informational sources in the library such as *Standard & Poor's Stock Guide, Value Line, Standard & Poor's Stock Reports,* etc. These books will give you a synopsis of what the company does, its sales and earnings and its stock price over the past few years. Using that informa-

Figure 6.1   Potential Investments

52-Week High	Low	Company Name	Exchange	Price	Comment

tion, you can either cross the company off your potential-investments list or add it to your second list (see Figure 6.2).

The stocks on the investment-grade list will need further research. You will want to use all the techniques described in the previous chapter to analyze these stocks. Once you have carefully analyzed the investment-grade companies and eliminated those that don't qualify, you should have a group of quality, low-priced stocks from which to choose your investments.

Over-the-Counter Stocks

Buying and selling stocks that are listed on the Over-the-Counter market is different from buying and selling stocks listed on the New York and American exchanges. While stocks listed on the NYSE and ASE are quoted with just one price, OTC stocks have a bid and asked price. If a stock is listed as $1 bid and $1.25 asked, this means that if you wanted to buy the stock you would pay the $1.25 asked price. If you wished to sell the stock, you would receive the $1 bid price. The $ .25 difference between the bid and asked prices is called the spread.

The spread on an OTC stock can indicate how actively the stock is traded. If a stock has a small spread, say $ .03, then it trades a lot. However, if a stock doesn't trade very much, in many cases the spread will be large. It is not uncommon to see a thinly traded stock with a $ .50 bid and a $1 asked. As an investor, you don't even want to consider a stock with such a large spread. Because you would have to pay $1 to buy and get only $ .50 if you sold, the stock would have to move up $ .50 or 100 percent before you break even.

Whenever you are considering an OTC stock, always check the spread. Avoid all stocks with spreads greater than those listed in Table 6.1.

OTC Pink-Sheet Stocks

Investments especially attractive to small investors are pink-sheet stocks. When a broker tells you about a great little company selling for only $ .75 per share, many investors say, "Gee, the stock is so inexpensive. What the heck, what can I lose?" Unfortunately, you can lose your whole investment.

Many pink-sheet stocks may seem low-priced but are actually tremendously overpriced! That $ .75 stock may have a $ .25 spread, which

Figure 6.2   Investment-Grade Stocks

52-Week High	Low	Company Name	Exchange	Price	Comment

is outrageous. In addition, pink-sheet stocks do not list a 52-week high and low price, so it is very difficult to discover if the stock is near its high or low. Often a pink-sheet company has a stock value of $50 million (number of shares multiplied by stock price), yet it does not have the $2 million in assets to become listed on the NASDAQ. To me, that indicates the stock is vastly overpriced.

Two questions you should always ask when a broker calls you about an OTC stock are:

1. Where is the OTC stock traded? If the stock is traded on the National Market System or NASDAQ, that's great. If it is a pink-sheet stock, say "thanks, but no thanks."
2. Where is the stock's current price in relation to its 52-week high and low price? Most investors fail to find out the answer to this question and wind up purchasing a stock at its high price. This can lead to disillusionment and selling at a much lower price.

A pink-sheet stock gets its name from the color of the pages of the National Quotation Bureau's publication that gives its bid and asked prices. Thousands of stocks do not meet the more stringent requirements to get listed on NASDAQ and are therefore listed on the pink sheets. There are five major problems with pink-sheet stocks:

1. The vast majority of penny-stock scams are pink-sheet stocks. Not all pink-sheet stocks are bad; however, they are the lowest rank of stocks. Basically, if a stock doesn't have the assets to get listed on any

Table 6.1   Target OTC Stock Spreads

Stocks between $ .125 and $ .25	$ .03 spread
Stocks between $ .26 and $ .75	$ .03 to $ .06 spread
Stocks between $ .75 and $2	$ .06 to $ .125 spread
Stocks $2 and up	$ .125 to $ .25 spread

of the more prestigious exchanges, then it falls into the pink-sheet category. A pink-sheet stock may have a great story about all its potential; however, I personally can't think of one pink-sheet company that has become a major corporation.

2. It is difficult to get any written information (including financial data) about the company. A pink-sheet company does not have to give shareholders financial information for it does not report to the SEC.

3. You can't check the company's price yourself. You won't find it listed in any newspaper. You can't call any broker to access the price on his or her computer. Normally, the only way you can find out the price is to call a broker who has received the printed pink sheets (which are yesterday's or last week's prices). In most cases, you must rely on the broker who sold you the stock for the price quote. Because the broker knows there is practically no way you can check the price quote, the broker may be tempted to quote what he or she thinks you want to hear rather than what the actual price is.

4. Another problem with pink-sheet stocks is that because they are not widely traded, there may be a big spread between the price you pay to buy the stock and the price at which you can sell it. In many cases, you pay 50 percent more to buy and that means your stock has to increase by 50 percent before you break even.

5. Not only do pink-sheet stocks have wide spreads, generally only one brokerage firm controls the market for that stock. If that brokerage firm goes under (which is not that uncommon), there may be virtually no market for the stock and the investor may end up with nothing except a worthless stock certificate. One such brokerage firm was the very successful Investor's Center, which had 27 offices across the United States and employed almost 1,000 brokers. A couple of years ago, Investor's Center closed its doors and left thousands of investors holding millions of dollars of stocks that were traded only by the Investor's Center. In 1990, the NASD and SEC entered into a major campaign to severely restrict brokerage firms that specialize in penny stocks. This was the final straw for many firms. Blinder Robinson filed for Chapter 11 and Stuart James closed down, leaving their customers without a market to sell their millions of dollars' worth of penny stocks.

Penny-stock brokers can make a tremendous amount of money in stocks that have large spreads. A major disadvantage of pink-sheet stocks is typically only one major brokerage firm makes a market in that stock. Consequently, that firm can easily increase the spread and give itself a bigger profit. It is not uncommon for a penny-stock broker to buy 100,000 shares of a pink-sheet stock for $ .02 from an investor who wants to sell and turn around and sell those 100,000 shares for $ .06 to an investor who hasn't done his or her homework to check the bid and asked. A cost of $ .06 a share sounds good and because the investor is buying from a market maker, he or she doesn't even have to pay a commission. Foolish investor!

Out of the $6,000 that the investor is paying to buy the shares, $4,000 is profit that will be divided by the broker and the brokerage firm. Only $2,000 actually goes toward purchasing the stock. In addition, because the bid is only $ .02, the stock will have to go up 200 percent for the investor to break even.

I believe a smart investor should buy stocks that are at least listed on the OTC NASDAQ system. This is a computerized system that provides brokers and dealers with the security's price at the touch of a finger when the company's stock symbol is typed into the system. To be listed on the NASDAQ system, a company must meet the specific qualifications of having at least $2 million in assets and capital and a surplus of at least $1 million. If a company has a stock symbol and is listed on the NASDAQ system, then you know it is a reporting company, which means it must send its shareholders quarterly and annual reports. There is one other OTC category—the National Market System. Stocks that are listed on it are the elite of the OTC market and are listed daily in every major newspaper.

THREE CRITERIA FOR SUCCESSFUL STOCK PICKS

When I decided to specialize in quality, low-priced stocks, I wanted to discover the best way to analyze these stocks to weed out the speculative investments. After years of studying fundamental analysis of blue-chip stocks, I have modified those methods of analysis for low-priced stocks. This successful technique for picking bargain stocks contains three criteria that a stock should meet to have the most profit potential:

1. The stock should have good sales.
2. The stock should have increased earnings (profits).
3. The stock should be near its 52-week low price.

In February of 1990, I recommended Tandon Corporation at $ .75. The company had posted a good increase in its third-quarter sales of $83 million, up significantly from $57 million the previous year. The net income was $2.2 million or $ .04 per share compared to a loss of $12 million or ($ .22) per share a year earlier. This was Tandon's first profitable quarter in more than a year. In addition, the $ .75 price was near its 52-week low price. In six months, Tandon's stock price had soared to $4 or + 433 percent!

Increasing sales and earnings show that there is demand for the company's products and that it can cover the additional costs to expand facilities to continue its growth. More importantly, increasing earnings (profits) indicate that the company is successfully marketing its product. Year after year of increasing profits signify that the company has the potential to move from a blue CHEAP stock to a blue-chip stock. The low stock price is the most important factor. Because most stocks are cyclical, moving from near their 52-week low to near their 52-week high, it just doesn't make sense to buy them when they are at the high point. I heartily disagree with brokers who call their clients and tell them about a great stock that is setting new price records and recommend that they buy it at the new record price because "it should continue to go higher."

It is not uncommon to analyze a stock and determine that it is a good investment, yet decide the stock price is too high. If that's the case, you can check the stock price occasionally. When it moves down, you can reexamine the company to make sure there is no negative news causing the stock price to drop. If there isn't, then you have a great investment opportunity—a quality company at a low price. These three factors are very important to the success of your investment. Having the patience and discipline to wait to purchase that quality stock near its 52-week low should guarantee a potential profit about 80 percent of the time.

LITTLE COMPETITION MEANS
VERY HIGH PROFITS

In just about any business environment, a company that offers a good product with little competition will be extremely prosperous. Perhaps one reason I have been so successful recommending quality stocks under $10 is that there is very little Wall Street competition.

Most analysts and brokers with major brokerage firms ignore stocks under $10. The majority of their recommendations are for stocks $15 and over. At the other end of the spectrum, there is a lot of competition in the highly speculative penny stocks and pink-sheet stocks. Investing in quality stocks under $10 is often forgotten and left to the few of us who are smart enough to recognize the potential.

When a good quality stock is at $2 or $3 a share, Wall Street usually doesn't get excited about it until it has moved up above $15. One such company was Dento Med Industries. In 1983, I recommended Dento Med at $1.25. The company had patents for two unique products used by the dental profession and it had great profit potential. At that time, no one else was interested in the stock. It had to move up to $15 before a major brokerage firm recommended it.

Dento Med eventually hit a high of $29.50 before splitting two for one. Investors who waited for their brokers to call them with the recommendation at $15 made a nice profit at $29.50 of 97 percent. However, if they had bought it at my $1.25 recommendation, they would have made a 2,260 percent profit! Dento Med illustrates how the investor can be the big winner by purchasing a quality, low-priced stock before Wall Street becomes interested in it. Dento Med had already moved up 1,100 percent from my $1.25 recommendation by the time the major Wall Street firm recommended it at $15. It pays to keep your eyes open for good investments.

HOW TO FOLLOW YOUR STOCKS

In the introduction, you learned how to read a stock page. Following your stock involves checking the price at least once a week or more if the stock is volatile. There are several ways you can get a price quote. Of course, if the stock is listed in *The Wall Street Journal, Investor's Daily* or your local newspaper, you can study it every day. You can call your broker for a price quote, but he or she won't appreciate it if you frequently call when the market is open and prevent your broker from making a commission. Unless you are considering selling the stock, I suggest calling for a quote after the market has closed.

You can also take advantage of a 24-hour telephone quote service offered by Charles Schwab and other brokers. You must have an account with Schwab and you may be required to trade a certain number of times to use the service. You should also contact your broker to see if the firm offers a stock-quote service. However you do it, it is important that you follow the prices of your stocks so you don't miss any opportunities to make a profit.

CHAPTER

┌─────────┐
│   │
│   7   │
│   │
└─────────┘

Mastering New Issues

The goal of many entrepreneurs when forming a company is eventually to take it public by offering shares of its stock to the public. This is the entrepreneur's opportunity to become rich, powerful and well known, and it must be immensely satisfying to open up the morning paper to check the price of *your company*. This is a part of the American Dream. Going public is a great opportunity for the entrepreneur, the company, its employees and its investors.

THE NEW-ISSUE PROCESS

To better understand what you are getting when you purchase a new issue, let's start at the beginning of founding a company to look at the aspects of going public and issuing stock.

Entrepreneur's Dream

Most companies begin with an idea for a new product or service or a better way of offering an existing product or service. The founder (or entrepreneur) establishes the company to fulfill that idea. Usually, the founder has enough capital or is able to borrow enough from family and friends to get going. However, when additional capital is needed to expand research and development, production or marketing, the company offers a new issue of stock to obtain the needed capital.

Business Plan

One of the most important documents that a company will prepare is its business plan. In essence, the plan is a map that the company intends to follow to successfully bring its product or service to the market. The business plan must have an appreciation of present realities and must follow a logical course of action, including the capital and resources needed. It should take into account the overall industry, trends, potential problems and direction. It should also include company characteristics, its balance sheet, the caliber of its management and specific company goals.

The business plan is vital because it is the first document that any bank, venture-capital firm, investment banker or underwriter will request when a company is seeking to raise capital. Let's assume that King Arthur Winery has achieved good sales and earnings by selling its wine for six years in the Midwest; however, it wants to expand its market to the West Coast. An aggressive expansion of its market will cost King Arthur Winery a tremendous initial investment. The company doesn't have enough capital for the expansion so it decides to raise the capital through a public offering of a percentage of its stock. This is an important decision and the advantages and disadvantages of going public should be carefully analyzed.

As explained in a previous chapter, going public is one of the easier ways and sometimes the only way to get needed capital. The public offering puts a value on the company and can be used as an incentive to attract or motivate key personnel. Once the company has public shares, it can use them as collateral when additional capital is needed.

However, there is a negative side to offering a new issue. It is expensive to issue the stock and keep the shareholders up to date. Once public, the company (except for pink-sheet stocks) is obligated to file reports with the SEC, which greatly increases paperwork and legal expenses (as much as $100,000 per year). The company loses privacy for now the shareholders have a right to know everything that can affect the company's success. It also loses control over some major decisions, such as mergers, and there is increased pressure for better sales and earnings.

Once the King Arthur Winery has carefully weighed both the pros and cons and decides to go public, it must locate a brokerage firm that is willing to underwrite its new-issue stock.

Underwriter

An underwriter is a brokerage firm that acts as the intermediary between the company issuing new securities and the investing public. The underwriter (or investment banker) either by itself or as part of a syndicate (two or more underwriters) agrees to purchase a new issue of securities from a company and distribute it to the investors. A major consideration of the new issue is what percent of the company should be given to the public for the amount of capital the company wants to raise. Let's say that the underwriter and King Arthur Winery decide that it needs to give up 50 percent of the company to raise $3.5 million for the market-expansion program.

Once the agreement is reached, the company and the underwriter sign an agreement. The agreement represents the underwriter's commitment to purchase the securities and King Arthur Winery agrees to pay all expenses incurred in preparing the stock issue for resale, including the costs of registration with the SEC and preparing, printing and distributing the prospectus.

Structuring the Deal

The underwriter will determine how much money the company can raise and at what price the shares should sell. Once a value has been given to the new issue, there are many combinations of shares and prices. For example, if $3.5 million is to be raised it can be offered for several different prices:

Number of Shares	×	Price	=	Amount Raised
350,000		$10.00		$3,500,000
700,000		5.00		3,500,000
1,000,000		3.50		3,500,000
3,500,000		1.00		3,500,000
7,000,000		.50		3,500,000
14,000,000		.25		3,500,000
35,000,000		.10		3,500,000
70,000,000		.05		3,500,000
350,000,000		.01		3,500,000

The underwriter, using expertise gained from previous new-issue offerings, determines the price that it believes will be most advantageous for selling the new issue. The price of the stock then will define how many shares will be offered.

Registering with the Securities and Exchange Commission

There are two SEC registration forms. The S-18 is filed by a company raising up to $5 million and the S-1 is filed when the company intends to raise more than $5 million. Although the SEC is headquartered in Washington, DC, there are several SEC offices throughout the United States and a company wanting to file an S-18 or S-1 will send it to the nearest office. An investor who wants to investigate a company or an individual connected with the company can use the SEC library at any of the regional or branch offices. SEC offices are located in New York City; Atlanta; Chicago; Fort Worth; Denver; Washington, DC; Los Angeles; San Francisco; Seattle; Philadelphia; Boston; Miami; Detroit; Houston; and Salt Lake City.

Most investors mistakenly believe that the SEC protects them from new-issue frauds. While the SEC reviews the registration statement of a company, it *does not have the authority* to pass judgment on the worth of the securities of that particular offering.

Many investors assume that if a new issue is registered with the SEC, the SEC checks out the company and gives it an approval. That is totally wrong.

The SEC has *no power to prohibit an offering* because it considers the investment opportunity to be a poor risk. The sole thrust of the Federal statute is the disclosure of relevant information. No matter how specula-tive the investment, no matter how poor the offering, it will comply with Federal law if all required facts are disclosed. In essence, as long as a company fills out the registration forms correctly, the SEC must *allow* the company to sell its securities.

Red Herring

After the registration statement is filed with the SEC, a waiting period begins before the final approval of the registration. Normally, it takes at least 30 days for the SEC to review the filing. However, the waiting per-iod could be much longer if the SEC has received many registrations. Usually at the end of each quarter, there is a rush of filings, which can delay the review.

In the interim, the underwriter can give prospective investors the preliminary prospectus or red herring (so named for the red ink on the cover page of the brochure). The red herring offers financial details about the issue or statutory prospectus; however, parts of the document may be changed before the final prospectus is issued.

Prospectus

Once the company has satisfied all SEC requirements and made any changes required by the SEC, it can then have the final prospectus printed. This document is supposed to be given to investors before the offer or sale of securities can be made. I recommend that all investors carefully read the prospectus before making a decision on the investment.

SEC law states that investors in a new issue must be sent a prospectus and must have time to read it before purchasing the security.

No matter how good the broker makes it sound, take time to read about the company. You may save yourself a lot of money and ag-gravation.

Filing in Individual States

After the company files its registration form to offer a new issue with the SEC, the underwriter must apply directly to each state in which the un-derwriter desires to sell shares. Virtually all states have a form of the blue-sky law, which was written to protect the citizens of that state from securities frauds.

The term *blue sky* originated from a famous 1915 case in which Justice McKenna asserted that a particular stock offering had as much value as a "patch of blue sky." The blue-sky law requires sellers of new-stock issues to register their offerings and provide financial details on each issue so investors can base their judgments on relevant data.

However, some states' blue-sky laws are so restrictive that almost all new issues fail to meet their stringent requirements. How does this affect you? An underwriter cannot legally sell shares of a new issue to an investor unless that investor is a resident of a state in which that new issue is registered. If you live in a state with very restrictive blue-sky laws, it may be virtually impossible for you to invest in any new issue before it goes public.

Types of New-Issue Offerings

When an underwriter buys a new issue from a company, it must decide how confident it is that the new issue will sell. Based on that confidence, the firm will either underwrite the new issue as a *firm-commitment* or *best-effort* offering.

The best type of new-issue offering is a firm commitment. The term means the underwriter is putting its reputation and company on the line. The underwriter is committing to purchase *all* the new-issue securities for sale to its customers. If all the shares are not sold, the underwriter is obligated to pay the company and hold the unsold shares in its own account.

> **Example:**   If an underwriter gives King Arthur Winery a firm commitment for its new-issue offering of 3,500,000 shares at $1 each, the underwriter is guaranteeing that the company will receive $3.5 million (minus commissions) whether it sells all the shares or not.

The second and more speculative type of new-issue offering is called a best-effort offering. This is an agreement between the underwriter and the company that the underwriter will act as an agency to sell the shares, promising to apply its best effort in selling the new issue to its customers. However, no guarantee is given that the offering will succeed. Usually, there is a minimum/maximum number of shares listed in the prospectus.

For the new-issue offering to go through, at least the minimum number of shares must be sold or all monies will be returned to the investors. This means that the company issuing the securities doesn't get its needed capital and has spent tens of thousands of dollars in legal fees, printing costs, time expended, etc., for nothing. Even though this sounds pretty grim, the vast majority of best-effort new-issue offerings do succeed.

Example: The underwriter has set a minimum of 2,000,000 shares and a maximum of 3,500,000 shares at $1 for King Arthur Winery. If the underwriter is able to sell 2,000,000 or more shares, then the new issue will go through. If the underwriter is unsuccessful in selling the 2,000,000 minimum, then the investors will have their money returned.

When the investor buys new-issue stock from the underwriter, his or her money is put into an escrow account until the new issue actually goes public and starts trading. Because the underwriter has 90 days in which to sell the new issue and can get a 90-day extension, it is possible for the investor's money to be tied up for six months or more. Why buy from the underwriter then? Because in many cases, the purchase price of the new issue immediately jumps up once it goes public and is offered on the secondary market. In addition, by purchasing a stock from the underwriter at the new-issue price, the investor pays no commission.

Underwriter Syndication and Support of the New Issue

In most instances, when an underwriter contracts to take a company public, the syndication department recruits other brokerage firms to take part of the new issue (see Figure 7.1). Working together, the brokers in the selling group market the shares to their customers and, once it goes public, continue to support the new issue with investors who will buy the stock in the aftermarket (secondary market). Doing so will create an orderly and fair market for the stock.

The selling group continues to promote and support the new issue after it goes public by offering the stock to more customers when the stock is on the secondary market. Because of the number and diversity of the brokerage firms involved, more investors become aware of the stock and the group of potential investors in the company is vastly increased.

Figure 7.1 Underwriter Syndication

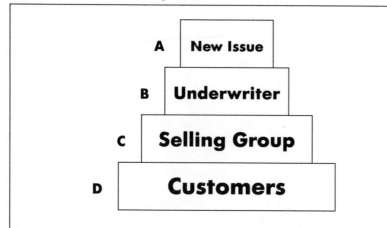

A The company sells its new issue to an underwriter.
B The underwriter syndicates a portion, perhaps up to 60 percent, of the new issue to other brokerage firms, which is known as the underwriters'syndicate or selling group for the new issue.
C The brokerage firms in the selling group create an interest for the new issue by bringing it to the attention of their customers.
D The customers invest in the stock, creating a market for the new issue.

That's the scenario I like to see. However, when a new issue is a penny stock that will have no stock symbol when the stock goes public and usually has only one underwriter, the scenario changes (see Figure 7.2).

Because the underwriter does not syndicate the new issue, the underwriter can better control the price of the stock. However, the market has been artificially created and the stock price may plunge when the underwriter moves on to its next new issue.

Major firms usually derive a small percentage of their total sales from new issues. However, many penny firms obtain the majority of their total sales from underwriting new issues. The more brokers involved in a new issue, the better chance for good support of the stock in the aftermarket.

An important new-issue term is *quiet period*. This usually is a 90-day period after the effective date when no new information is allowed to be released about the company. For the purpose of maintaining an orderly aftermarket, the SEC requires the quiet period to regulate public statements by the company.

Figure 7.2   Penny-Stock New Issue

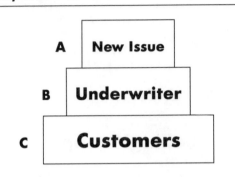

A   The company sells its new issue to a penny-stock underwriter.
B   The underwriter keeps the whole new issue and creates an interest in the stock through its clients.
C   The customers invest in the stock, creating a market for the new issue.

If the company has some very good news to release during the quiet period, such as a new contract or agreement with a major company, it can petition the SEC for permission to release the information. If the SEC OKs the petition, the company can add a sticker to the front page of the prospectus that contains a brief outline of the news. From the legal point of view, *a broker, newsletter or newspaper can only report information that is included in the prospectus when promoting a company offering a new issue.*

However, this rule is often violated, especially by penny-stock brokers who tell their customers information not contained in the prospectus, such as future plans or a contract or agreement that should be completed in the near future. Sometimes the future plans or contracts do materialize, but often they don't. Believe only what is written in the prospectus and you won't be disappointed.

HOW TO EASILY READ A NEW-ISSUE PROSPECTUS

Whenever you are looking to purchase a new issue, the *first* step you should take is to read the new-issue prospectus. If a broker calls you with an "unbelievable investment opportunity" in a new issue, don't just take his or her word; insist that the broker send you a prospectus. By law, a broker is not allowed to sell you a new issue before you read the prospectus, but an unscrupulous broker may "forget" that you haven't seen one.

The prospectus is a formal, written offer to sell securities. It contains information that a potential investor needs to make an informed investment decision. The prospectus describes the company's business history, operations, management's background, financial data, pending litigation (if any) and plans, including the use of the proceeds from the new issue.

Once you receive the prospectus, *don't be intimidated by all the legal terminology*. Reading a prospectus, especially the first time, can be a real chore. However, if you follow the highlights that follow, you should be able to quickly learn what the new issue has to offer and to determine if the security is one in which you want to invest. Every prospectus is slightly different, so items mentioned here may not be found in the prospectus you are reading. Take a look at our sample prospectus title page for King Arthur Winery in Figure 7.3.

An explanation of Sections A through H in Figure 7.3 follows, starting from the top of the page:

Section A   In this section, the total number of shares or units (combination of shares plus warrants) that the company is offering to sell to the public is listed.

Section B   This section provides the name of the company that is offering shares or units to the public.

Section C   If the company is offering a unit, this section tells what the unit consists of. It also gives details of the value of the shares and the warrants. It sets the warrant's exercise price and expiration date. (See Chapter 10 on warrants for further details.)

Section D   This statement, an SEC-required summary of the risk factors, is included in *every* prospectus.

Section E   This is a disclaimer stating that the securities have not been approved or disapproved by the SEC. In addition, while the SEC has required that the company follow the correct procedure in filing for the public offering, the SEC is not guaranteeing the accuracy of the information contained in the prospectus. This statement is also included in *every* prospectus. In essence, the SEC does not check out any new issue to determine if it is a good investment. What the SEC does is to make sure the company "follows the rules" for filing the new issue.

Figure 7.3 King Arthur Winery Prospectus

A
B **3,500,000 Units**
C # KING ARTHUR WINERY

Each Unit Consisting of One Share of
Common Stock and Two Warrants
to Purchase a Share of Common Stock

King Arthur Winery (the "Company") is hereby offering 3,500,000 units (the "Units"), each Unit consisting of one share of the Company's common stock, $.01 par value (the Common Stock") and two Common Stock Purchase Warrants (the "Warrants"). The Common Stock and the Warrants will be separately transferable immediately after the date of this Prospectus. Each Warrant entitles the holder to purchase one share of Common Stock at a price equal to the initial offering price of the Units commencing on March 31, 1992. The Warrants expire two years from the date of this Prospectus and are redeemable upon 45 days' written notice by the Company at $0.50 per Warrant beginning 30 days after they become exercisable. For more detailed information regarding the Warrants, see "Description of Securities."

The initial public offering price per Unit will be $1.00. Prior to this offering (the "Offering"), there has been no public market for the Units, the Common Stock, or the Warrants. There is no assurance that an active trading market will develop or be maintained following the Offering. The initial public offering price of the Units and the terms of the Warrants were determined by negotiation between the Company and W. K. Mathews Securities, Inc., the representative (the "Representative") of the several underwriters of the Offering (the "Underwriters"). See "Underwriting."

D THE SECURITIES OFFERED HEREBY INVOLVE A HIGH DEGREE OF RISK AND THEIR PURCHASE SHOULD BE CONSIDERED ONLY BY PERSONS ABLE TO SUSTAIN A TOTAL LOSS OF THEIR INVESTMENT. SEE "RISK FACTORS."

E THESE SECURITIES HAVE NOT BEEN APPROVED OR DISAPPROVED BY THE SECURITIES AND EXCHANGE COMMISSION, NOR HAS THE COMMISSION PASSED UPON THE ACCURACY OR ADEQUACY OF THIS PROSPECTUS. ANY REPRESENTATION TO THE CONTRARY IS A CRIMINAL OFFENSE.

F

	Price to Public	Underwriting Discounts and Commissions	Proceeds to Company
Per Unit	$1.00	$ .10	$ .90
Total	$3,500,000	$350,000	$3,150,000

G ## W. K. MATHEWS SECURITIES, INC.
1000 N. MICHIGAN AVE.
CHICAGO, IL 60601
H The date of this Prospectus is January 6, 1991

Section F The table shows the price of the new issue ($1 per unit), the commission the underwriter will receive for selling each unit ($ .10) and the actual amount of proceeds the company will receive from each unit ($ .90). It also shows the extension of this information for the total offering.

Section G This is the name and address of the underwriter from which you can purchase the new issue before it goes public. You can purchase the new issue only from that underwriter or other members in the syndicate of underwriters that are bringing the company public. Once the new issue goes public, you can purchase the stock from any broker.

Section H This section shows the effective date (the date when a registered offering may be sold to the public). Normally, the underwriter has 90 days from the effective date to sell the new issue. If the underwriter runs into difficulties selling the security, the underwriter may obtain a 90-day extension to complete the offering.

The first page of the prospectus tells quite a bit about the cost of the new-issue security and where you can purchase it. Inside the prospectus, you will learn about the company, its products or services, its goals, its marketplace and competition, the quality of its management and other factors important to the success of the new issue.

After checking the first page of the prospectus, turn to the Prospectus Summary (usually near the front of the prospectus). The summary outlines the most important information in the prospectus. It contains information about the following.

The Company This section details the company's background, business and products or services offered.

The Offering The offering explains the number of shares or units being sold. If units are involved, it specifies what each unit comprises. If warrants are involved in the offering, the exercise price and expiration date are stipulated.

Shares Outstanding after the Offering This part tells the total amount of shares outstanding, including the new issue. To determine what percentage of the company is being given to the public, divide the number of shares offered by the total number of shares outstanding. I like to see a company give 35 to 60 percent of its ownership in a public offering.

Example: If King Arthur Winery has 7,000,000 total shares outstanding and the offering is 3,500,000, then the winery is offering 50 percent of its company to the public.

Use of Proceeds   This explains in detail how the company plans to spend the money raised by the new issue. Many times the proceeds are used to pay off long-term debt, for the development of new products or as working capital. Look for a specific plan to expand the company's product or service or in the case of a development-stage company to bring its product to the market. The plan should state the amount of money to be spent at a specific time to implement the various stages of the strategy. If the prospectus is very vague about how the capital will be utilized, *stay away* from that new issue.

Hint: Avoid any new issue that plans to use the proceeds to repay loans from the management. The new issue is being used to benefit the company's management rather than the company itself.

Proposed NASDAQ Symbol   This is the company's stock symbol that will be used when the stock starts to trade. A smart company will plan ahead and obtain its NASDAQ stock symbol so that when it goes public, it can immediately be listed on the NASDAQ system. Many companies will try to select a stock symbol that relates to its business. For example, King Arthur Winery may choose the stock symbol *wine*.

Selected Financial Information   This section lists information about the company's finances. It usually includes sales or revenues, net income and net income per share for the past three or more years. This section should also give the total assets, total current assets, total current liabilities and stockholder's equity.

By reading the prospectus summary, you should be able to decide if the company has a good chance of being successful. If after reading the summary, you still believe it is a good potential investment, then you will want to check further by reading selected areas in the rest of the prospectus. Make sure you read about these areas.

The Management   Review the management's background to see if these people possess the necessary experience and knowledge to be an asset to the company. If the management's background experience is in completely different areas than the company's business, *be very careful.* Check to ascertain if the chairman of the board, president and vice president are spending 100 percent of their time with the company. If key management personnel are not devoting themselves solely to that company, *stay away*. If they have headed one or more public companies that ended up in bankruptcy, *do not invest*.

Litigation   Be sure the company is not involved in any major lawsuits that could seriously affect its business.

Management Compensation   This section can help the potential investor determine if the management is weakening the company with huge salaries. I would rather see salaries below average with good bonus incentives when management achieves certain goals regarding increasing sales and earnings.

Risk Factors   The prospectus is filled with bleak and discouraging disclaimers that are required by the SEC. While the SEC is trying to protect potential investors by making sure that they understand all the risks involved in buying a new issue, it can frighten an investor away from a good investment. Once you have read a few prospectuses, you will recognize the disclaimers and take them into consideration without letting them discourage you from investing in a quality new issue.

MAKING AND LOSING MONEY IN NEW ISSUES

New-issue securities can offer great profit potential if the investor checks before investing. Many poor new-issue investments can be eliminated just by carefully reading the prospectus. Only buy a new issue at the new-issue price; otherwise you may end up paying an inflated price. This is a key factor that can determine whether or not you make a good profit. In many cases, once the new issue goes public and is allowed to trade on the secondary market, the price skyrockets. Investors who were unable to purchase a stock at $1 at the new-issue price may find themselves paying $2 for the same stock once it goes public.

Be aware that many new issues are very overpriced. Analyze the company as you would any other stock and purchase the new issue only if you would buy it at that price if it were not a new issue. Avoid new issues that do not raise at least $2 million. Even if the new issue is a development-stage company, the $2 million will guarantee the stock a listing on NASDAQ. Always make sure the new issue will be listed at least on the NASDAQ system. If the company plans merely to be listed on the pink sheets or the Vancouver Stock Exchange, *do not invest in it*.

The state in which you reside will determine whether or not you can purchase a new issue. Several states have relaxed blue-sky laws, allowing investors to purchase any new issue. They are New York, New Jersey, Florida, Illinois, Colorado, Nevada and Utah. Some states are very restrictive about new issues. It is virtually impossible to purchase a new issue if you reside in California, Wisconsin, Pennsylvania or Texas.

I believe that the restrictive states are making a mistake. While protecting investors from poor investments, these states also keep investors from buying some great low-priced stocks. Many times, a $1 new issue will not meet the criteria of those states and their citizens will be unable to purchase the new issue before it goes public. Once the stock has gone public and received the capital raised by the stock issue, then it qualifies for listing in Standard & Poor's, which automatically allows the stock to be bought by residents in most states. However, by that time, the stock price has already jumped from the $1 new-issue price to $1.75 or $2 or higher. I have recommended many new issues over the years that have been great investments. One in particular is CarePlus, a $1 new issue that went public in December of 1983. CarePlus provides home health care, catering to the acutely ill patient. The company offers many services, from laboratory tests, pharmaceuticals, nutritional feeding through a vein or tube to anticancer drug administration, intravenous organic drug administration and rehabilitation therapy. At the time I recommended CarePlus, I believed it was a growth industry as home health care would expand tremendously for it is much cheaper than hospitalization. The company didn't disappoint me. In January of 1991, it traded at $22, which gave my subscribers a nice 2,100 percent return.

Once you have determined that a new issue is a good investment (a quality company at a low price) and have purchased it, it is essential that you monitor your stock very carefully. Many times a new issue will skyrocket and then just as quickly fall back. If you get a good profit (30 to 50 percent), *don't be afraid to take that profit.*

CHAPTER

8

Mastering Stocks in Bankruptcy

One investment area that has been almost universally ignored by the media is investing in companies in bankruptcy. Perhaps the reason is that the term *bankruptcy* is so negative that most investors, brokerage firms and analysts don't even consider a company in bankruptcy as an investment. There has been insufficient research on companies in bankruptcy and very little information is readily available for the average investor. In fact, the only publication I know of that was written specifically about that subject was my book, titled *Successful Investing in Companies in Bankruptcy*. Copyrighted in 1986, it quickly was sold out.

One of the most exciting things I discovered when writing that publication was the great investment potential that companies in bankruptcy can offer. If you are confused about the bankruptcy process, don't feel lonely. To the average person, bankruptcy means liquidating all of a company's assets and going out of business. Bankruptcy can mean that. However, Chapter 11 of the Bankruptcy Law offers an alternative to liquidation through the reorganization of the company. Sure the company has major problems, but under Chapter 11, it is protected from its creditors while it reorganizes and conducts business and it may very well survive that difficult period of time.

In fact, one company that experienced the largest percentage gain during this past bull market was Envirodyne Industries, a Chicago company that was selling for $ .25 in 1981 when it was in Chapter 11. It successfully reorganized under Chapter 11 and was bought out for $80 per share (taking into consideration a two-for-one stock split). That's an incredible gain of almost 319 times the original $ .25 investment! (*The CHEAP Investor* didn't do quite that well, for the newsletter recommended Envirodyne in October of 1984 when it was at $2.81. Envirodyne was bought out at $80 by the former management group of Beatrice.)

Five other Chapter-11 companies that increased by several hundred percent from their original recommendation prices are Charter Company, Storage Technology, AM International and the Lionel and Wickes companies. The potential is there; the investor just needs to understand the bankruptcy process and how to analyze companies in Chapter 11.

The small investor can make quite a profit by investing in companies in Chapter 11 because as soon as Wall Street even hears the rumor that a company is on the verge of entering Chapter 11, it panics. The stock price plunges as everyone bails out and many times the price falls well below the true value of the company. After carefully analyzing the company to determine if it will be a survivor, the smart investor doesn't let this opportunity escape. He or she can purchase stock worth much more for just a fraction of the price that investors were recently paying for it.

Many companies have reorganized under Chapter 11 and emerged to become prosperous, vital enterprises. On the other side of the coin, not every company survives Chapter 11. Sometimes there is just too much going against a company and after all is said and done, the company still goes into liquidation.

The list in Figure 8.1 shows companies that succeeded or failed in Chapter 11. Some of the failures are well-known names. That is why it is imperative to understand the bankruptcy process and thoroughly analyze the company before you invest.

BANKRUPTCY (CHAPTER 11)—AN OVERVIEW

To fully understand Chapter 11, you must first learn what bankruptcy encompasses. Bankruptcy is defined as "the state of insolvency of a person or corporation." Very simply, it is the inability of a person or company to pay its debts. The Bankruptcy Law was designed to accomplish two main objectives: to protect the debtor (company filing bankruptcy) against any frivolous suits by creditors (companies or individuals having money owed to them) especially when the debtor is still able to recover and to provide a fair means for distribution of a debtor's assets among all creditors. The bankruptcy process establishes priorities among creditors and prohibits the debtor from favoring one creditor over another.

Figure 8.1 Chapter-11 Companies

Successes	Failures
Toys R Us	Diamond Reo Motors
Envirodyne Industries	W. T. Grant Company
Chicago-Milwaukee Railroad	Osborne Computer
Wickes Companies, Inc.	E. J. Korvettes
AM International	Sambo's Restaurants

The bankruptcy code contains several chapters. However, Chapter 7 and Chapter 11 apply to companies. Companies that suffer severe financial difficulties have a choice of liquidating (Chapter 7) or reorganizing (Chapter 11). Chapter 7 means selling all the company's assets and distributing the monies received from the sale to creditors. Chapter 7's big disadvantage for the creditors is that they usually receive only a small percentage of the money owed them. Common shareholders may receive only a few cents per dollar value of the share.

The *best* alternative to liquidation for the company, creditors and shareholders is filing for Chapter 11 to restructure the company's debts in the hope that it can reorganize, survive and prosper. Chapter 11 is the financial restructuring of a company after it has filed for protection from its creditors while it works out a plan to repay its overdue debt. The company normally files a reorganization plan within 120 days and its debts are usually frozen for up to three years until the plan is approved. The aim of reorganization is to allow the company to continue operations while it negotiates with creditors and to eventually return the company to financial health.

If the plan does not work, the company may be liquidated (Chapter 7) and its assets sold to pay the claims of creditors and shareholders. However, if the company succeeds, the creditors should be able to get most of the money owed them. In many cases, creditors have been very pleased with the settlements from large companies that have entered Chapter 11.

LOCATING COMPANIES IN CHAPTER 11

In general, the easiest way to find companies in Chapter 11 is to read the stock tables in your local newspaper, *The Wall Street Journal*, *Investor's Daily* or *Barron's*.

Figure 8.2 Major Companies Currently in Chapter 11

Company Name	Stock Symbol	All-Time High Price	52-Week High	52-Week Low	Last
vjAmes Dept. Store	ADD	$34.63	$10.63	$0.47	$0.63
vjChyron Corp.	CHY	$11.88	$2.88	$0.25	$0.34
vjCircle K	CKP	$18.63	$4.00	$0.44	$0.50
vjContinental Airline Hld	CTA	$51.50	$12.13	$1.00	$1.88
vjHeritage Entertainment	HHH	$12.88	$2.25	$0.50	$0.63
vjLone Star Indus	LCE	$41.75	$18.13	$1.88	$3.75
vjLTV	LTV	$26.13	$1.63	$0.50	$0.56
vjPrime Motor Inn	PDQ	$45.50	$24.75	$0.31	$0.50
vjPublic Service of NH	PNH	$30.50	$4.00	$1.75	$2.38
vjRaytech	RAY	$29.75	$2.88	$1.13	$1.38
vjTodd Shipyards	TOD	$41.75	$6.38	$2.38	$4.13
vjVestron	VV	$15.25	$1.38	$0.02	$0.04
vjWheeling Pitt. Steel	WHX	$40.13	$13.25	$2.38	$4.25

The vast majority of NYSE and ASE stock tables designate a Chapter 11 company by putting a "vj" before the stock name. However, *Investor's Daily* uses a "b" to designate a company in Chapter 11. If you also want to check the OTC stocks, companies in Chapter 11 are indicated with a "q."

If you look at a list of companies that only shows the stock symbols, you can still tell which companies are in Chapter 11. When a company files for Chapter 11, its stock symbol normally is changed by adding a "Q" before the symbol. By investing just 15 or 20 minutes in scanning the stock pages, you can gather a pretty good list of Chapter-11 companies. A partial list of some companies in bankruptcy is shown in Figure 8.2.

CHARACTERISTICS OF CHAPTER-11 SURVIVORS

Now that you have compiled a list of companies in Chapter 11, the next step is to obtain information about them so you can decide which ones may be good investments. Sometimes information on Chapter-11 companies can be extremely difficult to find. Contacting the company and requesting the annual and quarterly reports can provide good background information. Another great informational source is a copy of the reorganization plan that the company usually issues within three to six months after filing for a Chapter 11. The plan can be requested by calling or writing the company. However, a new trend has begun and many

Chapter-11 companies require a $50 to $100 fee for a copy of the reorganization plan (even if you are a shareholder). Therefore, you will want to eliminate any companies that do not have good investment potential before paying $50 or more for the plan.

Certain types of companies have generally proven to be good investments when they emerge from Chapter 11. There are always exceptions to the rule, but by looking for the following fundamentals, you can pare your list to a more manageable number of companies for in-depth research.

Companies with Huge Sales

Experience has taught me that the best types of Chapter-11 companies are those with annual sales of at least $300 million. Any time a company enters Chapter 11, there is a chance that it will fail and be liquidated. However, a company with sales over $300 million obviously has been around for a while and usually has built up huge assets. It has a greater chance of surviving because the easiest and quickest way for a company to get turned around is to sell off some assets to obtain the necessary capital to continue operations and/or to pay creditors.

On the other hand, a company that has only $50 million in sales and a $40-million debt, for example, is going to be hard-pressed to reorganize, pay its debts and still have enough capital left to operate the company. It is possible, but not so likely to happen. The investor should definitely stay away from a company that has more debts than sales. The chances that a company with sales of $400 million and a debt of $900 million will survive are practically nil.

Companies Listed on the NYSE

The New York Stock Exchange has the most stringent requirements for membership. If a company has been successful in the past (which a listing on the NYSE indicates), the chances are greater that it will have the ability and resources to be successful again. NYSE-listed stocks tend to have sales in excess of $300 million and are generally well known on Wall Street, which are tremendous assets.

Many times, a company on the NYSE will be delisted when it enters Chapter 11, so you will need to research to discover if it was originally listed on that exchange. (Checking a copy of *The Wall Street Journal* from a month or so prior to the company's entering Chapter 11 should show whether or not it was on the NYSE.)

Companies That Are Former "Darlings" of Wall Street

Another good candidate for successful reorganization under Chapter 11 is a former "darling" or Wall Street favorite. Many companies that had a stock price of $40 or $50 or more and were listed on the NYSE are great investment choices because they are already well known.

Another advantage of a former Wall Street "darling" is that, in most cases, some brokers will continue to trade in the stock. Therefore, the company will have at least a limited following that should help push the price upward when it emerges from Chapter 11. Companies that did not interest Wall Street before they entered Chapter 11 probably would be unable to generate much interest when they emerge from it.

One Wall Street "darling" was Storage Technology. The stock that sold as high as $40.38 was a leader in the computer data–storage industry. A couple of years later, the company filed for Chapter 11 and traded as low as $1. When the stock emerged from Chapter 11, it sold as low as $2 but quickly jumped to the $7 level because of its Wall Street following and its history of previous success.

Companies with Widely Known Names or Products

The most difficult hurdle for a new company is becoming known to the public and to Wall Street. A company that does not have a known product has an extra deterrent to surviving reorganization because it still has to sell its product. If a company's product is well known, that asset could make the difference between reorganization and liquidation.

Lionel Corporation is an excellent example. I recommended Lionel in May of 1983 at $3.25 when it was ready to come out of Chapter 11. Less than two years later, the stock was $14. Lionel's biggest asset was its name recognition. Almost everyone either had a Lionel train when they were growing up or knew someone who did. Once Lionel streamlined its operations and sold off unprofitable divisions, its product sales were enough to ensure the company's success.

SELECTING BANKRUPTCIES WITH
THE MOST POTENTIAL

Once the obviously poor Chapter-11 candidates have been eliminated, there are still several areas to check to find the company with the best chances of survival.

Companies That Change Management

Poor management has caused the downfall of many companies. No matter how good a company's products, if they are not marketed effectively and if the company is not run efficiently, it will eventually lose money and may be forced into Chapter 11. If the balance sheet is not turned around, the company will be forced to liquidate to pay its debts.

Hiring a new CEO, who many times brings his or her own management team, can be an important factor in the survival of the company. There are teams that specialize in turning around companies in or near Chapter 11 and if the team has a record of successfully reorganizing other companies, that's a big bonus. Because the new CEO brings his or her own people, this destroys all the old political alliances and allows the new team to measure products, divisions and employees on performance instead of on clout. The ability to impartially cut out the deadwood and sell unprofitable assets is imperative to the company's survival.

Another consideration is the way the new management team is compensated for its work. If the team is paid a small salary, but receives a large bonus and/or stock incentives for positive results, then it will strive harder to turn the company around. Perhaps this is because the team has a piece of the action and is being paid in direct proportion to the well-being of the company.

Companies That Become Profitable

A major criterion for successful investment in a Chapter-11 company is to follow the company's balance sheet until it shows a profit. Even if a company has several of the previously mentioned criteria going for it, if it does not recover enough to show a profit, the chances are very slim that it will survive. It is imperative to analyze the company's current balance sheet, which can be found in its latest quarterly report. Let's take a look at the example in Figure 8.3.

Figure 8.3 Sample of a Current Balance Sheet

	1991	1990
Sales	$4,872,000	$7,950,000
Income Continuing Operations	371,000	(820,000)
Income Discontinued Operations	716,000	(513,000)
Extraordinary Item—Tax Credit	394,000	—
Net Income (Loss)	1,481,000	(1,333,000)
Income Continuing Operations per Share	.02	(.05)
Income Discontinued Operations per Share	.04	(.03)
Extraordinary Item per Share	.02	—
Net Income (Loss) per Share	.09	(.08)
Shares Outstanding	16,652,551	16,510,741

When analyzing the turnaround of a company's balance sheet, there are a few terms that need explanation.

Sales (or Revenues)   This is the monetary payment received in exchange for goods or services, or from other sources such as rents, investments, etc. Don't be too concerned about a decrease in sales. In most cases, unprofitable subsidiaries have been sold and this would cause the sales to decline.

Income-Continuing Operations   This is one of the most important areas to check on a Chapter-11 company's balance sheet. It is vital because these operations have survived and will become the basis for the company's sales and earnings. Check the figures to determine whether or not the continuing operations have increased their income over the previous year. An increase is a positive sign that the company is on the road to recovery.

Income-Discontinued Operations   This nonrecurring item is shown on the balance sheet for writing off a product or division that is being discontinued. (Sometimes it is found under extraordinary item.)

Extraordinary Item—Tax Credit   This nonrecurring credit offers a direct dollar-for-dollar reduction in tax liability. When a company loses money, that loss becomes a positive factor when the company becomes profitable again because the loss is deducted from taxable income and the company pays less tax.

Figure 8.4 Balance Sheet after Issuing a Large Number of Shares

	1991	1990
Sales	$4,872,000	$7,950,000
Income Continuing Operations	371,000	(820,000)
Income Discontinued Operations	716,000	(513,000)
Extraordinary Item—Tax Credit	394,000	—
Net Income (Loss)	1,481,000	(1,333,000)
Income Continuing Operations per Share	.01	(.05)
Income Discontinued Operations per Share	.02	(.03)
Extraordinary Item per Share	.01	—
Net Income (Loss) per Share	.03	(.08)
Shares Outstanding	46,652,551	16,510,741

Example: Chrysler at one time experienced tremendous losses. When Lee Iacocca turned the company around and it became profitable, those losses came back on the balance sheets as a tax credit (or tax loss carryforward) and were deducted from taxable income. Approximately 30 to 50 percent of Chrysler's net income resulted from the tax credits. Therefore, a large amount of tax credits (losses) can be a big asset to a profitable company.

Net Income or Loss The final profit or loss after all costs, expenses and taxes have been deducted, net income may be misleading because it may contain profits from the sale of divisions or tax credits.

Per Share Per-share items are determined by dividing the continuing operations, net income, etc., by the number of shares outstanding.

Shares Outstanding This is the total number of shares that have been issued. When comparing net income per share or income-continuing operations per share with the previous year's figures, always make sure the shares-outstanding figure is approximately the same. Otherwise, comparing the per-share figures from one period to the next will be of little value.

Many times, companies in Chapter 11 will satisfy part of their debts by issuing more common shares. In the previous balance-sheet example, the number of shares is just about the same. However, if the company had issued 30 million shares more to satisfy its debt (which is not uncommon for a Chapter-11 company), then the per-share comparisons would be misleading (see Figure 8.4).

Note that the per-share items for 1991 have dropped drastically from the previous example. By issuing such a large number of shares, the company has greatly diluted the value of its current shares. Dilution of share value should be considered when analyzing any investment.

Companies with a Confirmed Reorganization Plan

The strategy to satisfy the creditors of a company in Chapter 11 is called the reorganization plan. It usually is a compromise between the Chapter-11 company and the creditors and may involve full or partial payment of debts in cash, securities or other financial incentives.

It is important to read the reorganization plan to determine if the company intends to issue many more shares of its securities to pay off its debts. If so, those new shares will dilute the value of the stock and the company may decide to use a reverse stock split as a "quick fix" to increase the stock price. I believe that a reverse stock split is very hazardous to the shareholders' wealth. Do not invest in a company that is planning to execute a reverse stock split. If you already own stock, consider selling it.

A company usually files a reorganization plan about 120 days after going into Chapter 11 and normally has to amend it at least a couple of times over the next two to three years. The goal is to confirm the plan of reorganization, which means that two-thirds of the creditors and a majority of the claims in a class agree to the plan. If the bankruptcy judge approves the confirmed plan of reorganization, then the plan binds all creditors and the company can emerge from bankruptcy.

During reorganization, there are periodical meetings between the debtor and representatives for the creditors. Each creditor representative tries to increase the amount of distribution that his or her group will receive, while the debtor tries to encourage a plan that will allow it to emerge as a successful, reorganized company with adequate funds to continue operations. Needless to say, there is a lot of discussion and compromising before any plan is confirmed. If no agreement can be reached, the company may still end up in liquidation.

A Chapter-11 company that has a confirmed plan of reorganization has passed a very important hurdle. The time element is important, too. One of the biggest mistakes a company can make is to come of out Chapter 11 too soon. Be careful of a Chapter-11 company that comes out after only one or one and one-half years. Most successful companies stay in Chapter 11 for around three years to take full advantage of the reorganization.

Example: Recently, I have noticed that some companies in Chapter 11 experience a quick price jump when the reorganization plan is approved. For example, Johns Mansville was selling for around $2 and when the reorganization plan was approved, the stock jumped by about 70 percent during the next week.

THE NEW TREND IN BANKRUPTCIES

Recent developments in the public and courtroom attitude regarding lawsuits have caused some companies to seek protection from creditors offered by Chapter 11 even though, according to their balance sheets, the companies may not really need to be reorganized.

Because the public has become so willing to sue over just about anything and the courts are awarding huge settlements, many companies are finding themselves in dire financial straits because of lawsuits resulting from marketing a defective product or a product found to cause problems that show up years after it was used.

One company that sought protection under Chapter 11 because of massive lawsuits and settlements was A. H. Robbins. Based in Richmond, Virginia, A. H. Robbins is a leading pharmaceutical company. It also is the manufacturer of the Dalkon Shield, an intrauterine device (IUD) that has been shown to cause infections and other injuries. Even though the Dalkon Shield was pulled from the U.S. market more than 14 years ago, burgeoning lawsuits from women who were injured by the intrauterine birth-control device forced the company to file Chapter 11. When Robbins filed Chapter 11 on August 21, 1985, there were more than 15,500 lawsuits and claims against it from use of the IUD.

Continental Airlines filed for Chapter 11 in the mid-1980s when its costs became too high to compete in its marketplace. By filing Chapter 11, the company no longer was required to honor contracts, including those with labor unions. Many unions consider this tactic union busting. However, it allowed the company to renegotiate lower wages for its employees. In return, the employees were able to keep their jobs instead of having to seek new ones because the business was forced to liquidate. It is ironic that after Continental cut its labor costs (in addition to many other cuts), it not only survived bankruptcy, but became a profitable major airline for several years until it again filed Chapter 11 in November, 1990.

A. H. Robbins and Continental employed the Chapter-11 laws for reasons other than the original intentions, which shows how changing times can affect the way legislation is utilized. I am not taking sides on whether these companies have stretched the protection of Chapter 11 too far. I do think it is interesting to see companies making use of Chapter 11 in their fight for survival and I foresee more companies utilizing Chapter 11 for a variety of reasons besides the original intent. Those companies should be treated like any other potential Chapter-11 investment and must be carefully researched.

A disturbing new trend in bankruptcies is the management sellout to its creditors. Chapter 11 was instituted to protect the company from its creditors while it negotiated its debt and tried to successfully reorganize. Smart management teams utilize Chapter 11's protection and the threat of liquidation to negotiate the debt down to $ .20 to $ .30 on the dollar. This strategy protects the shareholder's equity and allows the company to emerge from reorganization with more assets.

Recently, however, some management-team members seem to be more concerned with satisfying creditors to avoid liquidation and losing their jobs rather than safeguarding the shareholder's investment value and the company's health. Instead of negotiating to reduce the debt, occasionally they will actually pay off the whole debt and give interest to the creditors. The only way they can accomplish this is to offer the creditors shares in the company, which means issuing millions of new shares. This severely dilutes the stock value and shareholder's equity. In many cases, the original shareholders may end up with less than five percent of the newly restructured company. If you see this happening to a stock you own, *sell it immediately*.

CHAPTER

9

Mastering Turnaround Stocks

I greatly admire John Templeton, the "grandfather" of modern turn-around (or contrary) investing. In 1939, just after World War II started, Templeton called his broker and gave him a very unusual buy order. He instructed his broker to buy 100 shares of every stock on the NYSE and ASE that was selling for $1 or less. When the broker called back to confirm that he had bought all the stocks that were $1 or under, he mentioned that of course he didn't buy any stocks that were bankrupt. Templeton startled his broker by insisting that he also purchase the bankrupt stocks that were under $1.

In all, Templeton bought 105 stocks, 35 of which were bankrupt. After about four years, he sold those stocks for more than $40,000 or almost four times his original investment. Why did he buy those stocks? Templeton believed that the United States would eventually enter World War II and that would spur the economy and cause his 105 stocks to appreciate in value. The stocks were extremely cheap, yet the companies had to be high quality to meet the listing requirements for the NYSE and ASE. Templeton correctly assumed those stocks had good potential to turn around. Because of their low stock prices they could easily have greater percentage moves, which would far outpace the higher-priced stocks.

While I certainly don't recommend doing what he did, John Templeton became the most famous and successful money manager in the world. His Templeton Growth Fund is one of the most profitable of all time and today consists of a family of 52 mutual funds with $13 billion under management.

One goal that all stock investors have in common is to find a stock with the potential to be the next Xerox or General Motors. This is a fine goal though most investors will never achieve it. However, there is one investment area that can provide great profit and self-satisfaction—turnaround stocks.

WHAT IS A TURNAROUND STOCK?

A formerly high-priced, successful stock that has experienced hard times causing a drastic plunge in its stock price meets the first qualification for a turnaround candidate. However, as the name indicates, it also needs to overcome its severe problems and show potential to resume being a successful company. Companies that survive bankruptcy are considered turnaround stocks, but many companies can be turnaround stocks without entering bankruptcy.

Typically, a turnaround stock is promoted to an unrealistically high price with the expectations of higher profits due perhaps to a new product, service or acquisition. When it becomes apparent that the profits have not materialized or that the new acquisition, product or whatever is not going to be successful, the stock price takes a nosedive. The price keeps falling, eventually becoming only a fraction of its high price. While the stock was very overpriced at its high, it may be extremely underpriced at its low.

Telex Corporation— A Turnaround Stock

A company can also experience plummeting stock prices if it generates poor sales and earnings compared to previous quarters. Telex Corporation is a good example. Its stock quickly soared to more than $50 a share in 1980 as it became a favorite of Wall Street and was on the buy list of virtually every brokerage firm. The stock was promoted by Wall Street to the point that it was extremely overpriced compared to the company's actual value. When Telex experienced some huge losses, the stock price dropped like a rock. As the losses continued, so did the falling price until the stock hit a low of $4. Just as Telex was tremendously overpriced at $50, it was immensely underpriced at $4.

In September of 1981, I analyzed Telex at $4 and despite large losses, I realized that it had the potential to far outpace the Dow Jones Industrials. I included it on the Blue CHEAP Index and over the next five years the stock not only turned itself around, but its investors must have been extremely gratified to see it soar from the $4 level to more than $100 for about a 2,500-percent increase! (Telex was later bought out at about $70 per share.)

It is interesting to note that Telex was on the buy list of virtually every Wall Street brokerage firm when it was at $50 in 1980. However, 18 months later when it was at $4, it was considered a bad investment. The stock price had to really move up before it was again included on the majority of the brokerage firms' buy lists. Of course, by the time the stock hit $100, everyone wanted to buy it.

The Turnaround-Based
Blue CHEAP Index

After many years of developing my CHEAP philosophy (quality, lower-priced stocks can far outpace the higher-priced, blue-chip stocks), I created the Blue CHEAP Index in August of 1981 using turnaround stocks. I was extremely bullish as I believed that "Reaganomics" would prove to be a boon to the U.S. economy and the stock market. Out of the 27 NYSE stocks that I picked for the index, only one was profitable; the other 26 were losing money. However, I believed that as the economy improved, their stock prices would quickly rise.

Over the next six years, the stock market (and the Dow Jones Industrials index) went through the largest bull market in our history. However, the 27 low-priced turnaround stocks that I picked for the Blue CHEAP Index consistently outpaced those 30 extremely profitable and well-known blue-chip stocks that comprise the Dow by a margin of 3 or 4 to 1. It confirmed my belief that the small investor can do far better by investing in quality, low-priced stocks than in blue chips.

THE HUGE PROFIT POTENTIAL
OF TURNAROUNDS

A quality turnaround stock has the potential to soar. One major advantage of a turnaround stock compared to other low-priced stocks is it was previously at a much higher price and many analysts already know the stock. Name recognition (for either the company or its products) can make it easier for the stock to move up a second time.

As explained in the previous chapter on stocks in bankruptcy, panic causes the stock price to continue to drop to the point that it is very undervalued. Recognizing that the company has learned from its errors and reorganized to solve its previous problems, the investor can purchase the stock for a fraction of its true worth.

Chrysler Corporation is a good example of a turnaround stock. In the early 1970s when Chrysler was selling in the $40 range, everyone wanted to buy the stock. However, the company introduced a line of full-sized cars just in time for the Arab oil embargo that sent American car buyers scrambling to buy small cars. Chrysler lost $52 million in 1974 and in 1975 experienced its greatest loss ever—$259 million. The stock price plunged. With continuing losses, by the time the stock price fell to $9, it was assumed that Chrysler would go into bankruptcy. This assumption caused the stock to bottom out at $4 since no one wanted it. On November 2, 1978, Chrysler hired Lee Iacocca (the creator of the Ford Mustang) as its president. Iacocca made sweeping changes in Chrysler and in 1980 Chrysler received a $1.5 billion loan from the U.S. government. The rest is history, including Chrysler paying back the government loan long before it was due. It is ironic that at $4 no one wanted the stock, but as Chrysler's dramatic turnaround persisted and the stock rose to $45, suddenly everyone was clamoring to buy it. Today Chrysler is at $11.

Investing in a Quality Stock in a Depressed Industry

In a variation of the same theme, you can make money in depressed industries. Of course, the smart investor won't invest in just any stock. He or she will analyze companies involved in that industry, searching for one that has good growth potential. That way, the investor has the opportunity to make a profit as the quality company responds to the normal upward fluctuation when the industry makes a comeback.

For example, the gold industry experiences up and down fluctuations. If gold is at a very low price, then it should only be a matter of time before that price begins to rise. Locating a quality gold-mining company and purchasing its stock can be very lucrative. In 1979, gold was at $850 per ounce and people were standing in line at their banks to take money out of their savings to invest in it. By February, 1985, gold had fallen to $280 per ounce and everyone became afraid to invest in gold.

While I don't pretend to be a gold expert, I realized that $280 was an exceptionally low price for gold and that at some point the cycle would begin an upward trend. Therefore, I did my research and found Galactic Resources Ltd., which had developed a new process of heap leaching for extracting gold from ore. With the new process, it cost Galactic under $200 for each ounce of gold. I recommended Galactic at $3.75 in January of 1985. Everyone was so apathetic about gold that Galactic fell to $3.38. However, over the next two years, the stock soared to $28 or +647 percent and split two for one as gold rose to the $500 level.

After the 1987 crash, investors got scared. As analysts forecast another depression, hoards of investors bailed out of stocks and invested their money in "something solid," such as gold for around $500 per ounce. You guessed it. The economy was much healthier than the analysts thought. There was no depression and gold sunk to under $350 per ounce. I firmly believe the investor will do far better buying a quality, low-priced gold stock than investing in gold bullion as a commodity.

The Contrarian Approach

Individuals who invest in turnaround stocks or depressed industries are known as Contrarians. As the name implies, this investment philosophy calls for investing contrary to what most investors and Wall Street are doing. The Contrarian opinion is that if everyone is certain that something will happen, it won't. This is the art of thinking for yourself, not succumbing to the influence of the crowd. This thinking works in just about any market because human nature is the same everywhere.

In the marketplace, most investors wait until they see mass buying before purchasing the stock themselves. Likewise, they wait until they see mass selling before they get out. (And they wonder why they can't make money in the stock market!) J. Paul Getty expressed this logic in his book, *How To Be Rich*, when he wrote that an investor should "Buy when everyone else is selling and hold until everyone else is buying. This is more than a catchy slogan. It is the very essence of successful investment and accumulating wealth."[1]

---

[1] J. Paul Getty, *How To Be Rich* (Chicago: Playboy Press, 1965), p. 195.

IDENTIFYING AND SELECTING
A QUALITY TURNAROUND

How do you discover the few turnaround stocks that have the potential for good profits? It takes research.

Locating Turnaround Stocks

The easiest way to find possible turnaround companies is to check *The Wall Street Journal, Investor's Daily* or *Barron's*. Look through the stock listings for a large spread between the 52-week high and low prices. Locating a stock with a high of $53 and a low of $2.75 indicates that something drastic has happened to the company. It will take further research to determine what it was and if the company has possibilities.

Another way to locate turnaround candidates is to follow the daily percent losers for the NYSE. (At least in the beginning I advise that you restrict yourself to NYSE-listed stocks since they are the largest, most-profitable and well-known companies.) I like to follow the daily percent-losers column because some of the best turnarounds started out being listed in this column as their prices plunged. You can also review the weekly, monthly and year-end percentage losers that are listed in *Barron's*. Some very well-known companies have been listed in the percentage-losers column. Another area you may want to check is the earnings reports that are listed on a daily basis in *The Wall Street Journal*. Look for companies that have produced a profit after suffering previous losses. Over a period of time, you can accumulate a list of stocks that may be turnarounds and you'll become familiar with their names and how their stocks trade. The next step will involve research to weed out the bad stocks and find those select few that contain the elements for a tremendous stock-price move.

What To Look For in a
Turnaround Stock

In August, 1982, I researched Grolier, Inc., which was trading on the Philadelphia Exchange at $1.81 per share. Grolier was the world's largest publisher and distributor of quality encyclopedia and reference sets and a leading publisher of children's books and educational items. The company had previously been listed on the NYSE and traded as high as $30.

However, Grolier suffered huge losses and moved down from the NYSE to start trading on the Philadelphia Exchange.

Grolier attacked its problems and turned itself around. When I decided it was a great investment, the company had annual sales of $345 million with a net income of $1.31 per share, yet it was selling for only $1.81. Grolier had well-known products and improved sales and earnings; however, Wall Street had failed to realize what a gem the company was at that price. A little later, Grolier applied for relisting on the NYSE and the stock started to soar. Eventually, the company was bought out at $27.50 per share, giving investors a tremendous profit of 1,419 percent.

Another turnaround company was Tandon Corporation, a glamour stock being prodded upward by Wall Street during the early 1980s when it was selling for $35.25 a share. Tandon was the hard-disk manufacturer for IBM's personal computers. When IBM decided to produce its hard disks in-house, Tandon's stock plunged. In February, 1990, I recommended Tandon at $ .75 per share because the company had branched into manufacturing its own home computers. Tandon announced its first profitable quarter in more than a year with sales of $84 million up from $56 million and net income of $2.2 million or $ .04 per share compared to a loss of $12 million or $ .19 per share the previous year. Tandon's stock soared from $ .75 to $4 or +433 percent in less than six months.

Most investors, including many brokers, pick turnaround stocks strictly by price. While this is an important factor, it is not the only one. I like companies that have established, well-known products, sales over $100 million and a stock price at perhaps ten percent of its previous high price.

The most important element is the company's balance sheet. When a stock's price has plunged, typically it's due to unexpected, severe losses. These create negative cash flow, high inventory and large write-offs. It can take a year or several years for the company to correct the problems that caused the losses and turn around its balance sheet. I like to buy a stock that has increased its cash flow and cash position, has lowered its inventories and has shown a profitable quarter.

I prefer to wait for the release of the positive figures rather than buying earlier when the company's management projects it will produce a profitable quarter. This tactic was developed from experience when many projected profitable quarters never materialized. In addition, the profits must be from continuing operations, not from tax credits or extraordinary credits. If the company is profitable only because of a big tax credit or an extraordinary credit from selling a division, then it really hasn't experienced the turnaround. Its continuing operations will be the final factor in determining whether or not the company maintains its profitability.

Claire's Stores on the NYSE was another turnaround-stock recommendation. Through its stores called Claire's Boutique, it caters to women's fashion-accessory needs at very inexpensive prices. The boutiques are located in shopping malls across the country. Claire's Stores was trading for more than $15 per share until it experienced difficulties and declared huge losses. Wall Street reacted by bailing out and causing the stock price to plummet. In February, 1988, I recommended Claire's Stores at $3.75 for I saw a good financial turnaround with nine-month sales of $70 million versus $55 million a year ago and net income of $3.6 million or $ .18 per share compared to $ .1 million or $ .06 per share the previous year. Claire's Stores' stock continued to move upward and hit a 1990 high of $23.88 or + 537 percent.

TURNAROUNDS TO AVOID

Not all turnaround stocks are good investments. It is important to know which situations to avoid so you don't lose your money. Probably only about five percent of turnaround stocks are excellent candidates with good profit potential. Now there will always be exceptions to the rule, but on the whole, if a company has any of the following going against it, its chances of being a successful turnaround stock are severely limited.

Companies in Industries That Are Very Capital Intensive

It is hard enough for a company to turn around its sales and earnings, create assets and working capital and lower its debt; but when the company is in an industry that requires a lot of capital, this can be too much to handle. If the company is in the entertainment, high-technology medical-research and development, real-estate, health-care or other industry where a large amount of working capital is needed and it can't obtain the capital through sales, the company may be forced to issue more shares of securities or go further into debt. Either way, the shareholder value is negatively affected by dilution.

I discovered a good example of this when I recommended Wessex Corporation in August of 1987 at $2.50. The company owns and manages many health-care facilities in the southeastern part of the United States. When I recommended Wessex, it had just returned to profitability with a good increase in sales and earnings. The stock price did move up to $4.50 after the recommendation. However, Wessex started to show losses the following quarter and continued to raise necessary capital by going further and further into debt. That eventually caused the stock to fall. The last time I saw Wessex's stock, it was selling for pennies.

The entertainment industry takes a great deal of capital to produce films. De Laurentis Films on the ASE was, at one time, a major name in the motion-picture industry. Its stock sold for more than $35, but because it needed an extremely high amount of capital to continue producing films, De Laurentis' debt soared and finally caused the company to enter bankruptcy.

Companies in the real-estate and high-technology medical-research and development industries also need huge amounts of working capital. In most cases, their stock prices are several times the companies' book value. In particular, the book value for real-estate companies can be greatly exaggerated and unrealistic. During the 1970s when real-estate values soared, many companies involved in real estate watched their stocks rise. Those companies leveraged themselves on high-priced real estate, hoping the prices would go even higher. When overpriced real-estate properties plunged, so did the stock prices. One company that was hard hit was Southmark, a multibillion-dollar giant in the industry. Its stock sold as high as $26, but currently Southmark is in bankruptcy and its stock is selling at a couple of cents per share. High-technology medical companies invest huge sums on research and development and then still have to spend years testing their drugs before they obtain Food and Drug Administration (FDA) approval to sell the drugs to the public. Often the company will run out of money before it obtains FDA approval to market the drug to the public and generate income.

Companies That Offer High Dividends

This is a trap that catches many unsuspecting blue-chip investors. They get caught when they look through the newspaper for low-priced stocks paying high-percentage dividends. They don't realize that most of the time the dividend percentage is so high because the stock has suffered losses and its price has plunged. The dividend percentage (which is based on the previous dividend when the company was making more money) moves up in response to the lower price, giving a very false impression. Many times, the investors find a high-percentage dividend and don't research the stock to see whether it has the cash to pay the dividend. If the company's price has just fallen to a much lower level, the reason usually is huge losses and debt. Needless to say, those losses may prevent the company from paying any further dividends for a while. When the company suspends or totally drops its dividend, the stock price can plunge even further and the investor has lost all around.

Companies Affected by Foreign Currency

There are two types of companies that fall into this category. The first is a company that purchases all its products from foreign countries. Over the past few years with the rapid fluctuation of the U.S. dollar, companies have experienced huge losses just because the U.S. dollar's value has declined.

Savin Corporation is a major distributor of office copiers designed for the low- to medium-volume user. In 1985, Savin suffered a tremendous loss of $2.70 per share and its book value plunged to a negative $5 per share. In 1986, the company brought in a new management team that worked hard to restructure Savin's debt and dispose of nonproductive assets. The management team concentrated on Savin's core business while consolidating space and personnel and implementing improved controls and management systems. By the first quarter of 1987, Savin showed a profit of $903,000, up from a loss of $5 million the previous year. The company's stock reacted to the favorable results by moving up from $1.38 to more than $2.

However, all the management team's efforts were negated by the declining value of the U.S. dollar. Savin's main product is a group of plain-paper copiers manufactured by Ricoh in Japan. When the U.S. dollar began to drop, Savin's contract with Ricoh became more expensive. By the time the dollar dropped to the point that it was worth 125 yen, it had wiped out all the bottom-line benefits that the new management team had accomplished. As the dollar continued to fall, Savin's stock tumbled until it hit its current selling price of $ .06.

The second type of company to bypass is one that sells the majority of its products to foreign countries and is paid in foreign currency. The fluctuation in the dollar can severely affect the company's balance sheet and threaten its profits. Several years ago, Grolier experienced huge losses because it had a significant investment in Mexico and the peso was devalued. Luckily for Grolier, the company received the majority of its sales from U.S. sources and was able to survive the losses.

Companies That Are Recommended
as Hot Tips

Always be careful of tips from any source. Don't take anyone else's word that a turnaround (or for that matter any stock) is a great investment without doing your own research. If you are going to invest your hard-earned cash, it is worth the effort to ask the person with the hot tip to send financial and general information on the company for you to analyze.

Turnaround stocks can give the knowledgeable investor enormous profits if he or she takes the time to carefully research and analyze the stock. If he or she doesn't, the investor is destined to lose money in the long run.

CHAPTER

10

Mastering Warrants

In September, 1986, I recommended both the common stock and the warrant of Medco Research. At that time, the common stock was selling at $2.50 per share and the warrant was $ .75. Over the next six months, Medco's common stock moved up to $25.25 or +910 percent! That's very impressive. However, Medco's warrant moved from $ .75 to $22 or +2,833 percent.

> **Example:** If you had $1,000 to invest, you could have bought 400 shares of Medco's common stock and would have had a potential value of $10,100. At $ .75, you could have bought 1,333 warrants, which would have skyrocketed up to a $29,326 value. That's three times the profit.

In general, warrants sell at a very low price in comparison to the common stock. Many times, good price moves in the common stock can result in tremendous price and percentage moves in the warrant.

In July of 1990, Millfield Trading Company was selling at $4 per share and its warrant was at $ .50. Over the next six months, Millfield's stock moved from $4 to $14.63 or +265 percent. Meanwhile, its warrant skyrocketed from $ .50 to $13.63 or +2,625 percent!

Example: If you had $1,000 to invest, you could have bought 250 shares of Millfield's common stock and would have had a potential value of $3,500. At $ .50, you could have bought 2,000 warrants, which would have jumped up to a $27,250 value.

DEFINITION OF A WARRANT AND ITS VALUE

Many companies offering new issues will do so in units, which is the combination of one or more common shares plus one or more warrants. What is a warrant? It is the right (but not the obligation) to buy usually one share of common stock at a specific price until a specific expiration date. Warrants can be bought and sold the same as stocks. They do not participate in profits, do not pay dividends and offer no voting privileges. The warrant's value, if any, is derived from the upward price movement of the common stock.

CRITERIA FOR ANALYZING AND SELECTING WARRANTS

Before purchasing a warrant, it is important to make sure the company you are investing in is a high-quality and low-priced company. If the stock price is already near its 52-week high, your profit potential will be greatly reduced. Once you have determined that the company is a good investment and the price is right, then you can begin to analyze its warrants. When analyzing warrants, you must be concerned with three components:

1. Exercise price—the price at which the warrant is exercised to buy one share of common stock. In other words, this is the price you have to pay to get one share of common stock.
2. Expiration date—the date by which you must exercise the warrant. The longer the time period before the expiration date, the greater the opportunity for the stock price to move upward, making the warrant more valuable.
3. Volatility—the more volatile the common stock, the greater the chance the stock price will jump up, increasing the value of the warrant.

These three components can make the difference between a profit and a loss. If you buy a warrant with an exercise price of $3 per share and an expiration date of September 30, 1996, you are betting that the common stock will move significantly above its current price before September 30, 1996. The closer the exercise price is to the current stock price and the longer the time period before the warrant expires, the greater your potential for good profits. Of course, if the stock is volatile, the possibility for profits increases.

Perhaps the most important factor in purchasing a warrant is to choose a good-quality company whose stock is currently undervalued. The warrant price is totally dependent on the price of the common stock so it is vital that the common stock price is low and has a good potential to move upward. No matter how low the warrant price, don't buy it unless you also consider the common stock to be a good investment.

FACTORS THAT MAKE WARRANTS MOVE UP OR DOWN

When a warrant is about to expire, a company may try to raise its common stock price up above the warrant's exercise price. If investors can purchase the common stock through the warrant for less than it would cost on the market, then they will exercise the warrant that delivers capital for the company's use. It is not uncommon for the stock price to plunge after the warrant expires because the upward price movement was artificially created by the company.

Therefore, *the real money is made in selling a warrant—not in exercising it.* If a company wants to exercise a warrant that you own, say "thanks, but no thanks," and take your profit by selling your warrant.

Example: One bargain-priced stock jumped from $ .09 to $ .63 over a six-month period. The company decided to exercise its warrant at $ .50. In other words, investors could buy a share of common stock for $ .50 rather than the then current $ .63 selling price. The smart people took advantage of the opportunity and sold their warrants at huge profits. The not-so-smart people exercised their warrants at $ .50 per share only to see the stock fall from $ .63 to $ .20 in a matter of weeks.

Table 10.1 Millfield Listing

52-Week High	Low	Company Name	Closing Price
14⅝	4	Millfield Trading Company	7½
13⅝	½	Millfield Trading Wt	3¾

HOW TO FIND WARRANTS

The easiest way to locate warrants is to look through the stocks listed on the NYSE, ASE or OTC in the financial section of any major newspaper, *The Wall Street Journal* or *Barron's*. The newspapers list warrants under the company's common stock and indicate the warrants by a "Wt" after the name. Table 10.1 shows the common stock of Millfield Trading Company and Millfield's warrant designated by a "Wt" after the name.

Sometimes a company has more than one warrant. Then the warrant will be designated by a "Wt" with an "A," "B," "C" or the year of expiration after it. Table 10.2 shows Ford Canada's common stock and three warrants.

In most cases, a company's warrant will be listed immediately below the common stock. Occasionally, the warrant will be listed on another exchange, as shown in Table 10.3.

Warrants usually are included in a new-issue offering as part of a unit. When the unit starts trading, it can be broken into its components. If the unit was composed of one share of common stock and three warrants, it may look like Table 10.4.

When the warrant is either called in or exercised by the company, it will, of course no longer be trading. However, it will be listed for a while in the papers as shown in Table 10.5.

Table 10.2 Ford Canada Listing

52-Week High	Low	Company Name	Closing Price
152	96	Ford Canada	98
6¼	1¼	Ford Wt 91 (A)	1¾
3	⅝	Ford Wt 92 (B)	1⅛
8⅛	3	Ford Wt 93 (C)	5½

Table 10.3 Listings on Different Exhanges

52-Week High	Low	Company Name	Closing Price	Exchange
4¹/₄	1	AM Int'l	1¹/₄	NYSE
1¹/₄	¹/₈	AM Int'l Wt	³/₈	ASE
11⁷/₈	3³/₄	Rymer	5¹/₂	NYSE
3	⁵/₁₆	Rymer Wt	⁵/₁₆	ASE

Some NYSE warrants that are currently listed in the financial pages of *The Wall Street Journal* are in Table 10.6.

As you can see, the warrant price is extremely small compared to the stock price. When you have a certain amount of money that you want to invest, purchasing a warrant on a good undervalued stock can give you more buying power.

WARRANTS VERSUS OPTIONS

Many people have a hard time understanding the difference between warrants and options. They are similar, but with a couple of important differences.

A *warrant* is the right (but not the obligation) to buy usually *one share* of a specific stock for a specific price until a specific expiration date. The expiration date can be *several years* in the future.

An *option* is the right (but not the obligation) to buy *100 shares* of a specific stock for a specific price until a specific expiration date. A typical option will have an expiration date from *three to nine months* in the future.

The important element is the time limit. Because most investors who buy options or warrants are doing so to trade not to exercise them, once

Table 10.4 Unit Listing

52-Week High	Low	Company Name	Closing Price
2¹/₈	⁹/₁₆	HOH Water	⁹/₁₆
1	¹/₈	HOH Water Wt	³/₁₆
9³/₈	2	HOH Water Un	2¹/₈

Table 10.5 Listing of Exercised Warrant

52-Week High	Low	Company Name	Closing Price
5¹/₄	1³/₄	Max Er	4¹/₂
¹/₄	¹/₃₂	Max Er Wt	. . .

the warrants expire, they have no trading value. Therefore, it makes
sense that the more time you have to trade the security, the better the
chance of making a profit. I suggest purchasing warrants that have at
least two years remaining until the expiration date. An additional advantage of warrants is that the commission rate is usually much less than
that charged for options. The warrant is a more conservative investment
than the option.

Table 10.6 Sample NYSE Warrants

52-Week High	Low	Company Name	Closing Price
10⁷/₈	3³/₈	Bond	4⁵/₈
1	¹/₆₄	Bond Wt	¹/₃₂
86¹/₄	59⁵/₈	British Petroleum	77
14¹/₂	6	British Petroleum Wt	8¹/₈
44⁵/₈	24⁷/₈	Federal National Mortgage	35
29⁷/₈	11	Federal National Mortgage Wt	20
6⁵/₈	3	Global Marine	3⁵/₈
4⁵/₈	1¹/₄	Global Marine Wt	1³/₄
21⁷/₈	17	Hanson	18¹/₂
7¹/₈	3⁷/₈	Hanson Wt	4³/₈
9³/₈	4³/₈	Manville	4¹/₂
3³/₈	⁹/₁₆	Manville Wt	⁹/₁₆
4⁵/₈	2	Navistar	2¹/₈
1¹/₈	⁹/₂₆	Navistar Wt C	⁹/₆₄
4	1¹/₈	Pan Am	1¹/₄
¹⁵/₁₆	¹/₃₂	Pan Am Wt	⁷/₁₂₈
16⁷/₈	10¹/₄	Safeway	12³/₈
4⁵/₈	2¹/₄	Safeway Wt	2¹/₂

Generally, warrants have the potential for superior gains for a small amount of money. If you have found a quality, low-priced stock that you are considering as an investment, always check to see if it has any warrants.

CHAPTER

11

Choosing the Best Broker for Your Needs

Brokerage firms have come a long way from the days when they strictly bought and sold stocks for their customers. Today, almost any type of personal financial service is available through one kind of brokerage firm or another, including life insurance, real-estate partnerships, mutual funds, financial planning and even checking accounts. Selecting the best broker for your needs takes a little planning and effort, but it could be one of the most important decisions you make.

You must first decide what kind of investor you are and would like to be, and where you plan to go with your trading. Are you a novice? Do you want investment advice from your broker or would you prefer to pick your own investments? The answers to these questions will determine whether you need a broker who charges higher commissions, but offers investment advice, or if you just need the least-expensive broker available to execute your investment trade.

FULL-SERVICE VERSUS DISCOUNT BROKERS

There are distinct differences between full-service and discount brokers. The full-service broker offers personal service. He or she will recommend specific stocks or investment strategies tailored to your financial needs and the size of your account. A full-service broker normally has more services available to help inexperienced investors. In general, full-service brokers charge up to ten percent of the price of the trade with a $50 minimum commission. Certain full-service brokers may slightly reduce their normal commission fees to their larger clients. (A full-service broker usually receives no salary. Instead, he or she is paid about 30 percent of the total commission fee.) Recently, many full-service brokerage firms have tried to bring in more income by charging clients a monthly account fee, mailing fees and even trade-confirmation fees.

A discount broker buys and sells stock for you at a lower commission rate—typically 25 to 80 percent less than the full-service fee with a $35 to $40 minimum commission. (The larger the amount of the trade, the greater the discount.) Generally, he or she does not recommend specific securities or strategies and offers no individual investment counseling or financial planning. The discount broker won't care about your personal balance sheet and since he or she receives a salary instead of part of the commission fee, the discount broker won't solicit your business to increase his or her paycheck.

Over the past year, the discount brokerage industry has added services and increased commission fees. Firms such as Charles Schwab offer many extra services but they are near the higher end of the discount commission scale, charging five or six percent. This is still cheaper than full-service brokerage firms' ten percent. Many discount brokers have significantly raised their fees for trading lower-priced stocks. This increase has created a niche for a new type of brokerage firm called a deep-discount broker, which charges from $ .02 to $ .03 per share. Many of these firms offer the ability to punch in your buy or sell order over your home computer or touch-tone telephone. Deep-discount brokers offer the least amount of services but the best prices.

With the passage of time, certain discount brokerage firms have begun to offer more and more services. Typically, the more services that are offered, the higher the commissions charged to cover the costs of the additional services. As an investor, you don't want to pay higher commissions for services you won't be using. However, if you are inexperienced, it may be well worth the additional cost to get a broker who will help you make wise investment decisions.

FINDING, KEEPING AND
WORKING WITH A BROKER

Just as you would search for high quality and value in a new car or home, you also should shop around for a good broker. After all, you are going to trust the broker with your money, so you want to be sure he or she is honest and will give you profitable advice and service. If you are very knowledgeable about the stock market and know exactly what you want to buy and sell, then you basically want an "order taker" who will execute your trades and your main consideration will be commission. However, if you need more help in making wise investment decisions, then you will want to utilize the following information.

Locating the Right Broker for You

First you must find some good candidates from which to choose your personal broker. You can ask for referrals from friends who invest, your tax accountant or professional acquaintances who are involved in the market, such as your doctor or dentist. If you don't know anyone who can recommend a broker, you can refer to the list of brokerage firms (in Figures 11.1 and 11.2), which have excellent reputations for employing honest brokers. If you live in a larger city, many of these firms will have a branch office that you can locate by looking in your local telephone directory. If not, use the telephone number to call the brokerage firm at its main office. (Some brokerage firms frequently change their telephone numbers. If you try a number and it is no longer correct, you can call directory assistance to request the current telephone number.)

If you are calling a broker who was recommended, you should tell him or her: "John Smith gave me your name." You'll want to inquire about which types of investments he or she specializes in, indicate how much you want to invest, and request that the broker send you several ideas.

As a courteous client, you should call to interview your broker candidate after the market is closed. That way you won't be depriving him or her of the opportunity to make a commission from another client who wants to buy or sell stock.

If you are calling a full-service brokerage firm, you should realize that most firms have a "broker of the day" who takes calls from individuals who haven't asked for a specific broker. You'll need to ask that broker which investment areas he or she specializes in and discuss how much you have to invest. You can request that he or she send you some investment ideas for consideration.

Be careful of any broker who pushes you to buy immediately. (You want service not pressure from a broker.) Also avoid any broker who insists that you invest a minimum of $5,000 to $10,000 with him or her. (You want a broker who is willing to help you even if you only have $1,000 to invest.)

Figure 11.1   Full-Service Brokerage Firms

A. G. Edwards &
 Sons, Inc.
One North Jefferson St.
St. Louis, MO 63103
314-289-3000

Robert Thomas
330 SW Washington #206
Peoria, IL 61602
800-475-9090

Prescott Ball &
 Turben, Inc.
447 Madison St.
New York, NY 10022
800-223-0610

Bear Stearns & Co.
245 Park Ave.
New York, NY 10167
212-272-2000

Kidder Peabody & Co.
 Inc.
10 Hanover Sq.
New York, NY 10005
800-543-3371
212-510-3000

Prudential Securities Inc.
199 Water Street
New York, NY 10292
800-245-2630
212-214-1000

William Blair & Co.
135 S. LaSalle St.
Chicago, IL 60603
800-621-0687
312-236-1600

Merrill Lynch & Co.
World Trade Ctr.
 North Tower
New York, NY 10281
212-449-1000

L.F. Rothchild Uterberg
 Towbin
222 Broadway
New York, NY 10038
212-238-2000

Blunt Ellis & Loewi Inc.
111 E. Kilbourn Ave.
Milwaukee, WI 53202
800-558-1055
414-347-3400

Oppenheimer & Co.
Oppenheimer Tower
New York, NY 10281
800-999-6726
212-667-7000

Shearson Lehman
 Brothers Inc.
World Financial Center
New York, NY 10285
800-992-0039
212-298-2000

Dean Witter Reynolds Inc.
2 World Trade Center
New York, NY 10048
800-854-5454
212-392-2222

Paine Webber
1285 Ave. of the Americas
New York, NY 10019
800-333-4231
212-713-2000

Smith Barney Harris
 Upham
1345 Ave. of the Americas
New York, NY 10105
800-223-7712
212-399-6000

Once you have at least three broker candidates, you should interview each candidate and discuss in depth his or her design for handling your account. The broker will need to know how much you expect to have available for investments and what type of investments you want to make so decide these aspects before talking to the broker. If you are a small investor, don't be embarrassed. In 1980, a New York Stock Exchange survey found that 57 percent of all investors invest less than $5,000.

Don't be intimidated by an impressive office or a smooth sales pitch. Discuss your financial goals and investment capabilities completely with the broker. He or she should express interest in your financial status and your personal taste in investment strategies. Following is a list of some questions that you can ask your broker candidate:

Figure 11.2 Discount Brokerage Firms

Brown & Company
20 Winthrop Sq.
Boston, MA 02110
800-343-4300

Heartland Securities
208 S. LaSalle Street
Chicago, IL 60604
800-621-0662
312-372-0075

St. Louis Discount
  Securities
200 S. Hanley, Suite 103
Clayton, MO 63105
800-726-7401

Burke Christensen &
  Lewis Securities
303 W. Madison,
  4th Floor
Chicago, IL 60606
800-621-0392
312-346-8283

Kennedy, Cabot & Co.
9465 Wilshire Blvd.
Beverly Hills, CA 90212
800-252-0090
213-550-0711

Charles Schwab & Co. Inc.
101 Montgomery St.
San Francisco, CA 94104
800-272-5600
415-627-7000

Ira Epstein & Co.
626 W. Jackson
Chicago, IL 60606
800-284-6000
312-207-1800

Muriel Siebert & Co.
444 Madison Ave.
New York, NY 10022
800-USA-0711

StockCross
One Washington Mall
Boston, MA 02108
800-225-6196
617-367-5700

Fidelity Brokerage Service
161 Devonshire St.
Boston, MA 02110
800-225-1799
617-227-0346

Olde Discount
  Stockbrokers
751 Griswold
Detroit, MI 48226
800-626-PLAN
313-961-6666

Waterhouse Securities Inc.
44 Wall Street
New York, NY 10005
800-672-7300
212-344-7500

First National Brokerage
  Services
1822 Douglas St.
Omaha, NE 68102
800-228-3011
402-346-5965

Quick & Reilly Inc.
120 Wall Street
New York, NY 10005
800-221-5220
212-943-8686

Wall Street Discount
100 Wall Street
New York, NY 10055
800-221-7990
212-747-5100

Andrew Peck Associates
32 Broadway
New York, NY 10004
800-221-5873

Pacific Brokerage
5757 Wilshire Blvd.,
  Suite 3
Los Angeles, CA 90036
800-421-8395

Robert Thomas
330 SW Washington #206
Peoria, IL 61602
800-475-9090

1. "How long have you been in the securities industry? How long have you been with this brokerage firm? Where did you work before?"
2. "Where do you get investment recommendations? Do you research them yourself or rely on others?"
3. "Do you have any client references?"
4. "How many clients do you have? Are you readily accessible by telephone to handle my transactions?"

5. "What specifics do you look for before giving a buy or sell recommendation? What's your philosophy for profit taking?"
6. "How are the firm's commission fees figured? Are there any discounts? Are there any other charges for services or monthly fees?"
7. "What services are offered by your brokerage firm? Does it have in-house personnel to research and analyze companies and market trends?"
8. "What's the financial condition of the brokerage firm? (Ask for the latest annual and quarterly reports.) Is it a member of any recognized national stock exchange? Does it belong to the NASD and the Securities Investors Protection Corporation (SIPC)?"
9. "What do the monthly customer statements include?"

You're the only one who can judge whether the broker's services, investment guidance and commission fees are compatible with your own investment objectives. If you want to invest in stocks under $10 per share, make sure your broker is satisfied with buying low-priced stocks. Your goal is to find a broker who is honest, efficient, dependable and, most importantly, feels responsible about the capital you are investing.

If you are an individual who makes your own investment decisions, you will want to find a discount brokerage firm. Because the brokers at discount firms are basically order takers, you'll be more interested in the commission schedule. Contact several firms and ask for information about opening an account. They should send detailed literature explaining their services and commission fees. Comparing the information from each discount brokerage firm should give you the basis to make an intelligent decision as to which to use.

There's no law against having more than one broker. In fact, if you have only one broker, it's hard to gauge how well he or she is doing. Many investors employ two or more brokers who they use for different investments. You may also want to consider using a discount broker to execute your trades when you know exactly what you want to buy and contacting a full-service broker for help in picking other investments. (I believe it is very inconsiderate for an investor to buy a full-service broker's investment recommendation from a discount brokerage firm to save commission fees. If your broker made the recommendation, you should buy the stock from him or her.)

Beware of the Unethical Broker

As recent scandals on Wall Street have revealed, brokers (and some brokerage firms) are just as susceptible to dishonesty and prone to mismanagement as are any other professionals who routinely handle large sums of money. In headline after headline, we read about brokers who didn't resist the temptation to excessively trade a client's stocks for the additional commission fees. In some instances, brokers have "borrowed" from customers' accounts to invest in a hot tip or swindled clients by convincing them to invest in worthless stocks.

> **Example:**   A housewife wanted to recover a $900 loss on an investment. She gave her broker (who worked for a major firm) permission (she claimed it was unwitting permission) to trade extremely speculative uncovered stock index options on her behalf. Her risk became apparent on October 19, 1987 (Black Monday), when her broker called and told her that she now owed almost $170,000 on her options account that he had handled! An equitable settlement was finally worked out—however, most investors are not so lucky.

When you have found a broker with whom you feel comfortable, you should check with your local branch of the NASD to make sure that there have been no complaints or sanctions brought against him or her. (The NASD has an office located in each state, usually in the capital or major city. You can obtain its telephone number from directory assistance.)

It is easy for an unethical broker to take advantage of the inexperienced investor. He can charge the highest possible commission rates and say they are the best available. If the investor doesn't check his statement, he will never know if that's true or not. After you get your broker's fees for a particular trade, you can call a few other brokers and ask for their rates on the same trade. This can help you determine whether your broker is giving you a good commission rate. Of course, if he is giving you special advice, then even if his fees are higher, he may be well worth the additional cost.

Opening an Account

Before you make any transactions with your new broker, you will probably need to complete a new account form, which is required by the SEC. Figure 11.3 shows the questions most likely to be asked. While some of the questions may seem awfully nosey, they're for your protection. Your broker must know your financial situation to decide which types of investments would best fit your circumstances.

Figure 11.3 A Typical New Customer Account Application

Date _____   Branch Office Location _____

Type of Account:

_____ Individual   _____ Partnership

_____ Joint   _____ Uniform Gift to Minors

_____ Corporation   _____ Trust

Name _____
              Last   First   Middle Initial

Spouse _____
              Last   First   Middle Initial

Mailing Address _____

_____

City _____ State _____ Zip _____

Home Address (If different)_____

_____

City _____ State _____ Zip _____

Employer _____

  Address _____

  City _____ State _____ Zip _____

  Position _____

Telephone
Work _____ Home _____

Bank Reference _____ Account # _____

Estimated Total Annual Income ____ Joint _____

Estimated Net Worth _____ Joint _____

Number of Years Investing _____

Investment Objectives

_____ Speculative   _____ Mutual Funds

_____ Income   _____ Trading

_____ Stocks   _____ Bonds

Signature _____

              Social Security Number _____

Just because you have confidence in your broker, you shouldn't ignore your investments. After all, mistakes can happen, especially in the hectic day-to-day rat race of a brokerage house. However, if the same mistake (or mistakes in general) keep occurring, then you've found a bad broker and should terminate your relationship. Remember, the brokerage community is a free market and you are at liberty to move from one broker to another as you please.

If you feel uncomfortable with your brokerage house or broker, or feel you are pressured by them, don't feel guilty about taking your account elsewhere. Your financial future is at stake and that comes first. Never stay with a broker if your relationship ceases to be potentially profitable.

Taking Possession of Your Stock Certificates

While your broker will keep your stock certificates for you, I recommend that you request that the stock certificates be put in your name and sent to you. Granted, you will have to rent a safe-deposit box (if you don't already have one) to hold the certificates, but there are many advantages to this request. You can evaluate your broker's efficiency by how promptly you receive the certificates. (Three to six weeks is normal.)

Having the certificates put in your name should ensure that you receive the annual and quarterly reports along with press releases. If your certificate is kept in the street name, then your broker is supposed to transmit that information to you when he or she receives it from the company. Some brokers are very religious about sending these materials to stockholders; many aren't.

Perhaps the main reason to ask for your stock certificates is to avoid delays if the brokerage firm that is holding them goes under. Over the past few years, many brokerage firms (even some with fine reputations) have found themselves in financial trouble and have closed their doors. Investors are protected by the SIPC and they will eventually receive all monies and stock certificates that the brokerage firm was holding for them. However, it takes time to sort through all the company's books and forward the certificates and proceeds. It is possible for the procedure to take from three to nine months. During that time, the investor cannot sell his or her stock because he or she does not have the certificate.

Sometimes a broker may resist your request to have the stock certificate sent to you because the broker believes that if he or she has the certificate, you will sell the stock through him or her and that broker will get the commission. (If the broker has given you good advice and service, he or she deserves the commission.) However, holding the certificate yourself gives you the option to sell the stock at any time through any broker.

Locating a good broker can be a time-consuming process, but the wise investor will make the effort to find an honest, knowledgeable broker with whom he or she feels comfortable. Because the average investor does not fully understand the risks involved in investments such as options, commodities, futures and penny stocks, his or her broker is obligated both morally and legally to know the client and suggest investments suitable for the client's situation.

Your broker must be readily available for your calls. If he or she doesn't have time to take your orders during a regular day, imagine the type of service you would get during a crisis like the 1987 crash. Remember, a broker will give his or her best clients the best service. If you are a small investor, you need a broker who will work hard to service your account even if it is modest.

CHAPTER

12

How and When To Buy Stocks

Buying the right stock for the right price is the key to making a good profit. Unfortunately, most individuals spend too much time trying to determine where the market is going and not enough time analyzing if the current stock price is a good value. After investigating several stocks and determining that they are quality companies, the smart investor doesn't just enter a buy order at the market price. He or she takes the time to establish a target price near the 52-week low and waits for the stock to reach it.

How To Buy Stocks

After choosing the stock you want to buy, it is extremely important to completely understand the process involved in purchasing stocks.

The Size of Your Stock Order

You must determine how many shares of stock you want to purchase. The amount of money you have to invest and the price of the stock will limit the number of shares you can buy. Depending on the size of your investment capital, you should consider diversifying by purchasing three or more stocks. (If you are starting out with only $1,000 to invest, you will want to use it all for one stock. If you have $10,000, then you can easily diversify into two, three or four stocks.) I advise that you begin with smaller amounts until you are confident that you are investing wisely.

You should buy stock in a round lot, which is the standard trading unit for stocks and warrants. Round lots are sold by 100s. Therefore, you can purchase stocks in any multiple of 100, such as 100, 200, 300, 1,000, 1,200, etc. If you buy 1 to 99 shares, then this is considered an odd lot and usually you will pay a higher commission. In most cases, an investor buying an odd lot (say 75 shares) will end up paying an extra 1/8 of a point when both buying and selling the stock. If you want to purchase 275 shares, this would be bought in a round lot of 200 shares and an odd lot of 75 shares. Because of the increased commission fees, I recommend buying only in round lots.

Another consideration in buying stock is if you only buy a few shares, the commission fee can consume a good portion of your profit. Typically, the commission scale favors buying more shares and in most cases, the commission to purchase 1,000 shares of stock may be only two or three times as much as the commission to purchase 100 shares. Therefore, I suggest purchasing 1,000 shares or more if possible.

Type of Buy Order

Once you have determined what stock you want to buy and approximately how many shares you want, you must decide what price you want to pay. There's a couple of different ways you can enter your order.

Market Order   More than 80 percent of all stock orders are executed by market orders. Very simply, you call your broker and authorize him or her to enter your order to buy at the best price available at the time your order reaches the floor of the stock exchange (in other words, at the market price). Market orders are usually given top priority on the communication systems of most brokers and can usually be executed in just a couple of minutes. This occurs so quickly that the broker may ask you to hold on the telephone while he or she completes the transaction.

Limit Order   If you prefer to set a specific purchase price for the stock, this is a limit order. For example, you call your broker and find that the stock price is $1.75, but you wanted to buy it at $1.50. You can enter a limit order specifying the $1.50 price that you are willing to pay for the stock. On the other hand, if you like the $1.75 price, but don't want to pay any more than that, you can also enter a limit order specifying $1.75. The limit order can be good for the day, month or until executed or canceled. While the limit order can save you some of the purchase price, there is no guarantee that the stock will drop down to the price you have set and you may miss buying into it.

HOW TO BUY THE RIGHT STOCK
AT THE RIGHT PRICE

The purchase price of a stock will determine how much profit you will make. You can select a quality stock, but if it is currently selling near its high price, your chances of making a good profit are very small.

□   **RULE 8**   □

Consider the purchase price of a stock to determine your profit.

Most stocks are cyclical, they tend to go up and down in price, and normally only a tremendously positive occurrence would cause the stock to move a good deal higher than its 52-week high. Unless something drastic happens to the company, its stock will typically move up near the 52-week high, gradually fall near the 52-week low and then start back up again. Therefore, it is essential to set a target price near the stock's low and wait for the stock to meet that price before purchasing it. You also want a stock that shows at least a 100 percent spread between its 52-week high and low price, otherwise the stock price may not move enough to make it a good investment.

How do you determine the target price? Look at the 52-week high and low and compare it to the current price. For example, a stock is selling at $2 a share and its 52-week high is $8.75. Its 52-week low is $1.13. You might set a target price at $1.50, which is about 25 percent below the current $2 price and near the 52-week low. If the stock falls to $1.50, you purchase it and then when the stock moves back up to $2, instead of just breaking even, you are already ahead 33 percent.

Of course, there's no guarantee that the stock will go down to $1.50. However, I have found this technique to work about 70 percent of the time. When you are trying to buy a stock near the low point of its cycle, it is possible that the stock will go even lower after you purchase it. By setting a target price below its current price, you are at least partially protecting yourself. Buying your stock at the right price is a critical factor in maximizing your profits.

PATIENCE AND DISCIPLINE PAYS

You've found a great little company that has so much potential; your only problem is that its price is high. Now comes the difficult part. You have to ignore that money burning a hole in your pocket and wait for the stock to fall to your target price. This takes a lot of discipline and patience, but it pays in the long run.

□   # RULE 9   □

Being patient can pay off in profits.

I will sometimes follow a stock for a year or more before it hits the perfect combination of being a high-quality company with a low price. It takes discipline to wait for the right price, but this can make the difference between profits and losses.

Patience and discipline are certainly major factors in the difference between an average and an exceptional investor. One of the investment classes that I teach is a five-week course specializing in low-priced stocks. During the first class, I ask my students not to buy any stocks until they have finished the course and have a much greater understanding of that type of investment. By the fourth class, I ask the students if they have followed my advice and resisted investing in all the stocks we discussed as examples. They don't have to raise their hands; I can tell by the sheepish grins on their faces. Usually, one half of the students didn't have the discipline to wait.

Too many investors hear a story about a "great stock" and have neither the patience nor the discipline to check it out. Instead, they rush to buy the stock "before it soars" and are greatly disappointed when the stock turns out to be a flop. How many times have you had someone tell you about an unbelievable stock that is going to make you a lot of money if you invest? I know that I have been tempted by such stories. However, if I actually investigated the stock, it usually was a poor investment risk. Perhaps the main reason why boiler-room brokers are so successful sell-

Table 12.1 Typical Stock-Price Variation

Quarter	Amount Invested	Market Price	Shares Bought	Total Owned	Total Invested	Value
1	$1,000.00	$2.50	400	400	$1,000.00	$1,000.00
2	1,000.00	3.00	333	733	2,000.00	2,199.00
3	1,000.00	4.00	250	983	3,000.00	3,932.00
4	1,000.00	3.25	307	1,290	4,000.00	4,192.50
5	1,000.00	3.00	333	1,623	5,000.00	4,869.00
6	1,000.00	3.75	266	1,889	6,000.00	7,083.75
7	1,000.00	4.00	250	2,139	7,000.00	8,556.00
8	1,000.00	4.25	235	2,374	8,000.00	10,089.50

ing penny stocks, commodities, futures, worthless oil and gas stocks and other scams is because they know the average investor has no patience. Rather than exercising a little discipline to analyze the stock, the foolish investor gets so wrapped up thinking about the "money he or she can make" that the investor loses his or her good sense.

In my business, I get several calls each day from brokers or companies' officers telling me about how wonderful their stocks are. I have learned to never let a good stock story overwhelm my discipline. I always ask that information be sent to me so that I can analyze the stock myself before making any investment decision. This strategy has saved me a lot of trouble and money.

DOLLAR COST AVERAGING

Dollar cost averaging is among the simplest and oldest of all formula plans. Basically, it consists of investing a constant amount of money in stocks over a long period of time, regardless of the level of the stocks' prices. This technique allows an investor to realize profits as long as market prices fluctuate and the same dollar amount of investments continues to be purchased periodically.

For example, an individual has $4,000 to invest each year and buys $1,000' worth of a stock each quarter; as the stock price rises, fewer shares can be bought with the $1,000, and when the stock's price dips lower, more shares can be bought.

The example in Table 12.1 shows a typical variation in a stock's price. For dollar cost averaging to work, two ingredients are necessary.

First, the security prices must be volatile and the stock's price should be on an upward trend. Money cannot be made on a stock whose price shows a continuous downward trend. By diversifying your portfolio, this danger is greatly reduced.

Secondly, the investor must be willing and able to purchase securities of an equal dollar amount when stock prices are low as well as high. In a depression, salaries may be cut and the money available to follow the plan may be reduced or totally lacking at the very time when stock prices are at their lowest and, therefore, most-attractive level.

The success of dollar cost averaging hinges on being able to liquidate the portfolio when the securities' prices are high. The investor can increase big profit potential by planning to liquidate the portfolio several years before it is needed. Thus the investor can delay the final liquidation if the stock's price level is too low.

Buying securities through a monthly investment plan is a type of dollar cost averaging. It is also a great type of forced savings plan. The periodic buying of mutual-fund shares and regular contributions to a pension fund that invests in common stocks could also be classified as a type of dollar cost averaging program.

HOW TO AVERAGE DOWN

A major difficulty in purchasing stocks is that the investor has no way of knowing what low price the stock will hit before it turns around and starts its upward cycle. Unless you own a crystal ball that reveals that information, about all you can do is make an educated guess and hope you are right. However, there is a strategy that can prove useful.

When you purchase a stock, consider buying only half as many shares. Then if the price falls, you can buy more shares at the lower price and bring down your break-even point. The break-even point is the average price paid for all shares of stock. (If you bought 1,000 shares at $2.80, then your break-even point is $2.80.) Once the stock price moves above the break-even point, you are making a profit. Of course, before buying any more stock, you would first determine that nothing dreadful has happened to the company, causing the price to fall. After reanalyzing the company and concluding that it is only a normal price fluctuation, then and only then, would you consider averaging down.

For example, if you had $5,600 and wanted to purchase 2,000 shares of Storage Technology at $2.80 per share, instead of buying all 2,000 shares at once, you purchase just 1,000 shares at $2.80. This gives you some available cash to purchase more shares if the stock price falls. This happened after one of my Storage Technology recommendations. You could have purchased the first 1,000 shares at $2.80 asked, leaving $2,800 for further investment. Sure enough, the stock fell to $2 and if you bought at that price, your $2,800 would purchase an additional 1,400 shares. Table 12.2 shows how that would affect your break-even point.

By lowering your break-even point to $2.33, when the stock moves back up to $2.80, you have already made a profit of 20 percent!

Most investors make the mistake of putting all their cash into a stock so they don't have anything available to average down when the opportunity presents itself. Even if the investor does have some accessible cash, he or she usually will just invest in another stock rather than take advantage of averaging down and lowering his or her break-even point.

By the way, after Storage Technology moved down to that $2 price, it turned around and jumped up to $7 a share. If you had purchased the original 2,000 shares at $2.80, they would have been worth $14,000. You would have had an $8,400 profit or + 150 percent. However, if you had averaged down, you would have 2,400 shares for a value of $16,800. Your profit would have been $11,200 or + 200 percent!

Averaging down is the opposite of what most Wall Street brokers would recommend. They prefer to see their clients average up. Using the same example, you bought 1,000 shares of Storage Technology at $2.80. The stock moved down to $2 and then started back up. It passed $2.80 and when it reached $4, your broker recommended buying more, so your $2,800 balance would purchase an additional 700 shares. You now have 1,700 shares and if they were sold at the $7.00 price, your total would be $11,900. Your profit would have been $6,300 or 113 percent. This is quite a bit less than what you could have made averaging down. I advise to only average down. *Never* average up on your investments.

TAKING ADVANTAGE OF THE NEXT BULL MARKET

Many small investors will miss the next bull market because they follow the crowd. In late 1981 and in 1982, many stocks were extremely underpriced. However, most small investors hesitated to get into the market at that time. Instead, they waited until late 1986 and 1987 to jump on the bandwagon when everyone was talking about how much money could be made in stocks. Consequently, those investors bought stocks at extremely high prices, assuming that the stocks would continue to move

Table 12.2 Averaging Down Example

1,000 shares at $2.80 = $2,800		$5,600 divided by 2,400 shares =
1,400 shares at $2.00 = $2,800		$2.33 average price
2,400 shares	$5,600	

even higher. Unfortunately, October 19, 1987, dashed those hopes as the market plunged more than 508 points.

The institutions were the big sellers on October 19th. However, the small investor was besieged with a media blitz that forecasted the end of our economy as we knew it. Everywhere that the small investor turned, the "experts" predicted a major recession, perhaps even a depression. With such gloom and doom, it is no wonder that the small investor became scared and decided to bail out of his or her stocks the next day.

While the small investor was selling, all the institutions that had panicked the day before suddenly realized that the Dow stocks were now underpriced and these institutions started to buy. The market soared. Now the small investor was really confused. The media kept spewing out stories on the crash and the small investor decided to stay out of the market for a while. Even though the market moved up to more than 3,000 by July of 1990, the small investor was still sitting by the sidelines. Figure 12.1 shows the drastic drop in the number of small investors after the crash.

A few newsletter writers announced that they had forecast the crash and many small investors decided "those guys must know what they're doing" so these investors jumped on the writers' bandwagon. Many of the analysts who claimed to have predicted the crash did so because they always were pessimistic. Needless to say, they weren't about to change their strategy for predicting doom had worked before, so everyone ignored the great bargains. The brokerage industry suffered as sales dropped by 50 percent and the industry had to let many brokers go. This perpetuated the gloomy atmosphere. No one was looking at what the stocks were doing.

Three years after the 1987 crash, many small investors are still hesitant to buy stocks. While their attitude is starting to change, this is a slow process and the investors who missed out on the extremely underpriced stocks in the wake of the crash will probably be the ones who will miss the bargains after the Middle East crisis is settled. Make sure you're not one of those investors. By investing in quality, low-priced stocks, you'll be positioned to take advantage of the next upswing in the market.

Figure 12.1   Small Investors Since the Crash

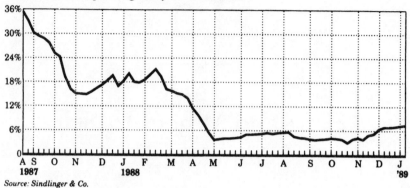

Small Investors Increase Buying Plans...
Percent of holders planning to buy more stock soon

Source: Sindlinger & Co.

CHAPTER

13

How and When To Sell
Your Stock

While no one *knows* the lowest price a stock will hit before it begins to move upward or the highest price it will achieve before starting to fall, the smart investor can use certain techniques to help buy or sell a stock at the best price. This chapter will give you some guideposts for obtaining a good profit.

"Cutting your losses" is a phrase that is commonly used by many Wall Street brokers, analysts and newsletter writers. They advise that if your stock price falls 10 to 20 percent, sell the stock to cut your losses. One well-known adviser recommends selling if your stock falls eight percent. I believe this advice can be foolish because many volatile stocks can easily fall more than that before soaring upward. If your stock price falls, you should take the time to review the company to learn if there has been any negative news that caused the price to drop. Sometimes if an investor sells a large block of stock (perhaps he lost his job and needed the cash), this can send the stock price tumbling even though the company is still in excellent financial shape. If there doesn't seem to be any valid reason for the decline in the stock price and it has dropped 25 to 30 percent, you may be wiser to average down.

Awhile ago, I watched Allwaste Corporation, which was recommended at $5.13, move down to $3.75, falling $1 in just one day. Several people called me and said that they had sold near $3.75 "before it went even lower." I just shook my head because the company really didn't have anything wrong with it. In fact, when I called the company to find out why it fell $1 in a day, I learned that an institution sold 300,000 shares at $3.75 (that it bought at $17 per share) just to get out of the stock. Within the next week, Allwaste had turned around and shot up to over $6. I'm sure those investors who got frightened and sold at $3.75 are kicking themselves because they missed out on an excellent profit opportunity.

TAKING YOUR PROFIT, PROTECTING YOUR PROFIT

A common investment fault is falling in love with your stock and never selling it. For example, the investor watches her stock price rise to the point where she has a good profit. However, she doesn't sell; instead, she watches the stock price fall back down again. The investor has forgotten that the main reason for buying a company's stock is to *make a profit!*

It's all right to love your company, but look at it another way. If you love the company so much, wouldn't you want to own more of it? You can if you are willing to sell when you have a profit and buy it back after the price falls.

If you have $2,000 and like a stock selling at $1, you can buy 2,000 shares. If the stock goes up to $3 and you take your profit and sell, you now have $6,000. Keep following the stock as it falls back down again to $1.25. After reanalyzing the company to make sure it still is a good investment, you can buy 4,800 shares with your $6,000. The company's stock continues on its upward cycle and hits $2.50. You sell the stock and now have $12,000, which gives you a $10,000 or +500 percent profit and allows you to purchase even more shares of stock when the price again falls near its low. You can love a stock, but don't let it blind you to making a profit.

Perhaps one of the most important things to remember when figuring your profit on an investment is to look at the price move in percentages rather than in points. If you don't, it is easy to get confused.

For example, you have $3,500 to invest and buy $1,500 of stock A, which is selling at $2 per share, and $2,000 worth of stock B, which costs $40 a share. You would be able to buy 750 shares of stock A and 50 shares of stock B.

$1,500 ÷ by $2 per share for stock A = 750 shares
$2,000 ÷ by $40 per share for stock B = 50 shares

If stock A goes up $ .75 and stock B increases by $5, offhand, it looks like stock B has performed better. However, if you actually figure out the profit percent, you will see a different story.

750 shares × $ .75 increase = $562.50 profit
$562.50 profit divided by $1,500 purchase price = 38 percent

50 shares × $5 increase = $250 profit
$250 profit divided by $2,000 purchase price = 13 percent

This example shows why it is important to look at your profits in percentages rather than just in points.

After purchasing a stock, the wise investor will spend a little time along with his money and check the stock's price in the local newspaper (if the stock is listed). If the stock hardly moves, checking the price every week may be often enough. However, if the stock is more volatile, it is a good idea to look at its price every day or so. For example, Oak Industries had been trading between $ .75 and $ .88 for several months and then in one week jumped up to $1.38. However, by the end of the following week, Oak had fallen to $1. If the investor didn't check the stock price, she could easily miss the opportunity to make more than a 50-percent profit.

TIPS FOR WHEN TO PLACE A SELL ORDER

From 1982 through 1986, we experienced a runaway bull market and it was easy to make a 100-percent profit or more on your investments. Recently, the market has been more volatile with wild upward and downward swings. Unfortunately, the upward movement of stock prices in general is not so great and if you have a 35- to 50-percent profit, you should consider taking it. There are certain telltale signs that can indicate the possibility that a stock's price will fall. The smart investor looks for these signs and takes them into consideration.

The Company Announces a Reverse Stock Split

One of the worst decisions a company can make is to execute a reverse stock split. Time and time again, I have seen that maneuver hurt instead

Figure 13.1   3-for-1 Stock Split

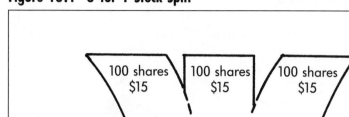

100 shares $15   100 shares $15   100 shares $15

Original 100 shares
at $45 per share

100 Shares × $45 per Share = $4,500
300 Shares × $15 per Share = $4,500

of help the stock price. To understand a reverse stock split, you must first learn about a forward stock split.

Forward Stock Split   A stock split occurs when a corporation's board of directors decides that the stock price is too high. Therefore, the company splits the stock price to make it more attractive to institutional buyers and other investors.

There are many possible stock-split configurations—1.5 for 1, 2 for 1, 3 for 2, 4 for 3, 5 for 1 and 5 for 2 are just a few. How does a stock split work? Figure 13.1 shows a 3-for-1 split. Before the stock split, 100 shares of stock were worth $45 per share. Once the stock is split, the 100 shares become 300 shares, each worth $15. If you multiply the shares by the price, you will see that the dollar value is the same, even though the number of shares is different. Why go through the bother of a stock split? Many companies split their stock to make the price more attractive to investors. The company's total number of outstanding shares also is increased by the stock split. If the company had two million shares outstanding before the 3-for-1 stock split, it would have six million shares outstanding after the split.

Table 13.1 Reverse Stock Split

	1-for-8 Reverse Stock Split			
	Company		Investor	
	Before	After	Before	After
Shares	32 Million	4 Million	4,000	500
Price	$1	$8	$1	$8
Value	$32 Million	$32 Million	$4,000	$4,000

Reverse Stock Split   A reverse stock split may occur when a company can't convince any Wall Street analysts or brokers to support its stock. Many times the excuse for the lack of support is that the stock is trading at too low a price. Most Wall Street analysts and brokers employed at the major brokerage firms will not even review a stock selling below $5. If a company's stock is selling at $1, the company has two choices. It can concentrate on the bottom line, increasing sales and earnings, which should slowly but surely cause the stock price to move upward. *Or* it can take the "quick fix" approach and execute a reverse stock split.

As you have probably guessed from the name, this is just the opposite of a forward stock split, so instead of ending up with more shares at a lower price, the reverse stock split creates fewer shares at a higher price. For example, if that $1 company has 32 million shares and decides to do a 1-for-8 reverse split (see Table 13.1), the company would end up with only four million shares at a price of $8 each. Likewise, an investor with 4,000 shares would have 500 shares after the reverse stock split.

In 11 years of recommending stocks, I have seen more than 20 companies execute reverse splits and more than 95 percent of them are lower in value today than before the reverse split. My statistics show that in almost every case, after a reverse stock split, the shareholders' value will decrease from 35 to 50 percent or more. Why does this happen? It's simple. One day the stock is selling at $1 per share and the next day it is selling at $8. There is a resistance factor involved. When a stock's price suddenly jumps up without any substantial gains in profits to bolster the price, the market, which has valued the stock at $1, resists the higher price, causing the price to fall. In addition, many specialists and traders are aware that reverse stock splits cause the price to drop and they use that to their advantage by shorting the stock, which also applies pressure on the price. Even the small investors can help drive the price down. They see that their stock has gone up in price (without realizing they have proportionately fewer shares) and they sell for a profit (they think). A large amount of "profit taking" can send the stock price tumbling, causing more selling.

This is true whether the company is listed on the pink sheets with no sales and earnings or is an extremely profitable company listed on the NYSE. Wickes Companies, Inc., is a prime example. NYSE-listed Wickes is extremely profitable, with more than $5 billion in sales, yet it couldn't successfully pull off a reverse stock split! In April of 1987, Wickes was trading at $4.63 per share and its management announced a 1-for-5 reverse split. The stock started to trade at $22.50, but almost immediately began to fall. In about five months, Wickes' stock fell to $7, creating a 70 percent loss in value for the shareholder.

I feel that a reverse stock split should be approached with extreme caution by the companies that are contemplating it and by investors who own or are thinking of buying stock. Over the years, I have seen the vast majority of reverse stock splits seriously erode shareholder value, along with damaging the management's credibility. Any time an investor hears that his or her company is going to execute a reverse stock split, he or she should immediately sell. If he or she really likes the stock, the investor will probably be able to buy more shares at a much lower price a few months after the split.

The Company Raises Cash
Through an Equity Offering

A company that needs working capital often will raise the money through an equity offering. The company can offer a portion of its equity through issuing additional common stock, preferred stock, rights, warrants, private stock and convertible or junk bonds. However, with each offering, the value of the company's existing shares will eventually be diluted by the additional shares. When a company completes such a financing, about 95 percent of the time its stock price falls. The larger the financing, the larger the dilution and, correspondingly, the farther the stock price will drop.

When a shareholder receives the quarterly report, he or she should check the amount of cash the company has. A drastic drop in the company's cash can signal trouble for the stock's price. If the company is in a cash-intensive industry such as the entertainment or high-technology fields, be very careful if the cash drops below $100,000.

To compare the company's cash position, you will need to refer to its annual or 10-K report. In the report's Consolidated Balance Sheet section, the Assets will list Cash and will show figures for two or more years. (Sometimes there also will be a Cash Equivalents column, which shows stocks or other investments. They should be considered as Cash when determining the company's cash position.) In the following example, the cash has radically decreased.

	1990	1989	1988	1987
Cash	$97,369	$4,680,274	$7,747,321	$10,346,837

These figures indicate that the company has been using about $3 to $4 million in cash each year for working capital. With only $97,369 at the end of 1990, the company will probably need to find a way to supplement its cash. If the company is to survive, it will have to obtain more working capital from sales, a loan *or* an offering of more shares through its investment banker.

If the company chooses to offer more shares, it will dilute the value of the existing shares and this usually will cause the stock price to fall. When the smart investor foresees the need for an offering, he or she can sell the stock. Most of the time, the investor can buy it back later after the additional shares have caused the stock price to fall.

Certain industries are not so cash-intensive and the company may not need such large cash amounts. Pacer Technology is a fine example of a company that usually averages $15,000 cash on hand. However, this works for Pacer because the company has no long-term debt and any expansion is financed from its sales. Perhaps the best strategy when comparing the cash position in previous years is to look for a drastic decrease. Further research should show if the decrease was caused by an acquisition (which could be very positive for the company) or from other more negative sources. By following the company's cash position, the investor can decide if the company will have to find some method of raising working capital and whether the investor should consider selling his or her shares.

Large Increases in Inventory Occur

While reading the balance sheet, also check the inventory position, especially if the company manufactures products. Many times a huge increase in the company's inventory indicates the start of trouble. When inventory builds up in the warehouse, besides the obvious fact that it isn't bringing in revenues, it also creates a drain in the company's finances for the expenses incurred by the additional inventory financing, warehousing, taxes and insurance. If the company's earnings have also dropped, this could mean serious problems on the horizon and the investor should consider selling the stock.

A Warrant Is about To Expire

Warrant holders won't exercise the warrant to purchase more shares of the company's stock unless the stock price is higher than the price the warrant offers. Some lower-priced companies that need the additional capital generated from the exercise of the warrants will promote their stock to artificially inflate the stock price above the warrant's exercise price so investors will exercise the warrants. After the warrant is exercised, however, the stock price usually falls because it was raised to an unreal level and there are now more shares outstanding and the stock value has been diluted.

The Company Merges with Another

When one company merges with another, typically the stock price jumps in anticipation of the merger and then comes down to the agreed-on price on the day of the official merger. The interest created by the merger news brings in investors, which raises the price, but after the merger, the interest subsides and so does the stock price.

In addition, combining the two newly merged companies may temporarily cause substantial increases in expenses. Personnel changes, reorganization confusion, etc., can cause disastrous reductions in profitability until the reorganization is completed and new personnel learn their jobs. Many times, the investor can sell the stock for a higher price just before the merger is completed and then buy it back at a lower price after the merger.

When a merger calls for the shareholders to receive one share of the new company for more than one share of the old, this is actually a disguised reverse stock split. For example, the shareholder must pay three shares of the old stock for one share of the new stock. Reverse stock splits usually are bad news for shareholders and they should sell. A few months later, the investor can usually purchase the stock at a price 35 to 50 percent less.

For example, when Robert Halmi, Inc., merged with Hal Roach Studios, the Halmi shareholders paid 2.5 shares of old stock for 1 share of the new company, which was to sell at $5. Several months after the merger, the stock was at $3 or 40 percent less. After many trials, tribulations and name changes, the stock is currently selling for $ .03 bid.

Another Company Buys Shares for a Much Lower Price

Normally, if one company buys shares of another company that is doing well, it would pay a higher price per share than the current market price.

When Homestake Mining bought one million shares of Galactic Resources, it paid $8.75 per share even though the stock was then selling at $5. Why didn't Homestake just buy the one million shares on the open market if the price was cheaper? If Homestake had tried to buy that many shares, it would have caused the stock price to jump up perhaps as high as $10 or $11 per share. Instead, Homestake contacted Galactic and worked out an agreement that was beneficial to both companies.

If your company agrees to sell a large number of shares to another company at a price that is well below the market price, beware. A CEO who agrees to sell shares for significantly less than the current price is signaling Wall Street that he believes his company's stock price is too high and the price the other company is paying is a more accurate reflection of what it should be.

If a company with great sales, earnings and growth is selling at $4.75 per share, but agrees to sell two million of its shares for only $2.25, Wall Street is going to assume that the company's management thinks it is only worth $2.25 and the stock will probably fall to that price in the near future. If the other company had purchased the two million shares on the open market, the stock price would probably have soared to $10. Any company that sells a large number of shares for a lot less than its market price is simply giving the company away and this is disastrous for the company's shareholders.

MARKET-SELL, LIMIT-SELL AND STOP-LOSS ORDERS

You invested time and effort to research several stocks to discover a quality company at a low price and now this has paid off. Your stock price has risen 200 percent and it is time to take your profit. You can call your broker to enter either a market- or limit-sell order.

Market-Sell Order

This is by far the most common type of sell order. Roughly 80 percent of all sell orders are market-sell orders. This type of order would offer your shares of stock at the best prevailing price (market price) as soon as possible after the order reaches the floor of the exchange. This is the quickest way to sell the stock and unless you are selling a large block, it should be executed that same day.

Limit-Sell Order

Investors who want to sell their stock for a particular price would use a limit-sell order. Very simply, this specifies a price and a time period during which the shares will be offered at that price. The limit order is only good for a day unless the investor requests that it be offered for another time period such as a week, month or "until canceled."

The shares may or may not sell depending on whether anyone wishes to pay the specified price. A limit-sell order may be canceled at any time and another entered at a higher or lower price depending on the circumstances.

If you bought ABC company at $1 and find the price has risen to $2, you can call your broker and enter a limit-sell order offering your shares at $2.25. However, if the stock has not been sold and, in fact, the price has fallen to $1.88, you can call your broker and cancel the sell order at $2.25 and enter a new one at whatever price you want. Because you don't want to lose your profit, you may want to enter a sell order at $1.88 or at the market price.

Stop-Loss Order

A smart investor will use a stop-loss order to protect a profit of 100 percent or more. Ideally, you call your broker and set a certain price at which the stock will automatically be sold if it falls that low. If used correctly, the stop-loss order is an excellent tool to protect your profit.

For example, if the ABC Company stock has risen to $2.25, the investor can enter a stop-loss order with his or her broker at $1.88. If the stock falls to $1.88, it automatically should be sold. If the ABC Company's stock price continues to move upward, then the investor would also raise the price at which the stop loss is set.

Figure 13.2 Setting a Stop-Loss Price

$5.25 ––– $4.88

$4.75 ––– $4.38

$4.25 ––– $3.88

Stock Price $3.75 ––– $3.38

$3.25 ––– $2.88

$2.75 ––– $2.38   **Stop-Loss Price**

$2.25 ––– $1.88

$2.00 ––– $1.63

$1.00 Purchase Price

There is a technique to using the stop-loss order. Remember, this is set to protect your profits. You don't really want to sell the stock because you believe it will continue to move upward; however, if it does start to fall, you won't end up back where you started (or worse).

Most stocks don't move straight up or straight down. In its upward cycle, a stock may rise 3/8, fall 1/4, rise 1/2 and fall 1/8. The stop-loss order has to allow some room for normal downward movement of the stock before it begins to rise again. In many instances, the even-dollar price ($2, $3, $4, etc.) becomes a base as the stock falls back that far and then starts upward. Therefore a stop-loss order should never be entered at an even-dollar amount. That is why in the previous example, the stop-loss was set at $1.88 rather than at $2.

As you can see, it becomes a delicate balancing act to try to preserve as much profit as possible if the stock does plunge; however, you also don't want the stop-loss price so close to the current stock price that the stock is sold just because the price dipped down before rising again. If the stock is especially volatile, the stop loss may need to be set slightly lower. Once the ABC Company's stock rises to $2.75, the investor would raise the stop-loss to $2.38. Avoid the $ .50 level for the stock could easily fall that far. Figure 13.2 shows suggested guidelines for setting a stop-loss price for a stock as it rises from $1.

It is possible that your broker cannot handle stop-loss orders. Most discount brokers don't offer this service. Also, if the stock is on the OTC market, your broker may be unable to enter a stop-loss. If you encounter this problem, you still can make use of this technique by setting your own stop-loss point and entering a sell order with your broker if the stock falls to that point. You will have to closely follow the stock price; however, this is worth the effort to avoid losing a good profit.

Don't confuse a stop-loss order and a stop-limit order. The stop-loss order protects the investor's profit by selling the stock if it goes down in price. The stop-limit order sets a high price at which the stock will be sold if and when it reaches that price sometime in the future. In addition, the stop-loss price is lower than the current market price while the stop-limit price is higher.

TAX SELLING AND THE JANUARY EFFECT

As the end of each year approaches, many brokers recommend that their clients check their portfolios to determine if they have any stocks that are in a paper-loss position. (The stock's current price is lower than the price at which the stock was purchased.) If their clients do, the brokers advise them to sell the stock and take the loss for tax purposes.

I disagree with the timing of that philosophy. Statistics show that most low-priced stocks are closer to their 52-week low price in November and December (probably due to other investors selling for a tax loss and driving down the price). Therefore, because the investor can sell for a tax loss at any time during the year, he or she would be much wiser to sell at the point that he or she determines that the investment has become unprofitable.

I believe that the investor shouldn't indiscriminately sell a stock for a tax loss without analyzing it first. Because low-priced stocks seem especially susceptible to the end-of-the-year falling price, if the company is a good investment and the price has just dropped, the wise investor should buy more shares rather than sell for a loss.

One thing to consider when selling stock for a tax loss is that if you are in the 28-percent tax bracket and you sell a stock in late December for a $1,000 loss, you only save $280 tax dollars. If the stock was a bad investment, fine, $280 is better than nothing. However, if the stock is a quality company, it could easily rise higher than the $280 tax credit after the beginning of the year. For example, Acclaim Entertainment hit a low of $3.25 in December of 1990 primarily because of tax selling. It soared up to $5.88 or +81 percent by mid-January of 1991. Investors who held on at the low price made more money than those who sold and received at most a 28-percent tax loss.

Tax selling causes the price of many stocks to drop. When other investors see the price of their stock falling, they panic and sell, causing the price to fall further and creating some excellent bargains. The individuals who sold for the tax loss now have money to invest. However, they wait until after the first of the year for tax purposes, which generates a corresponding upswing in price in January. This phenomenon, called the January Effect, normally results in low-priced stocks far outpacing blue-chip stocks.

Smart investors don't follow the crowd; instead they are Contrarians. They use the January Effect to their advantage and buy good-quality, lower-priced stock in early December when the prices have dropped and sell in January or February for a good profit. Using the Contrarian approach at any point can be very profitable.

☐   Rule 10   ☐

Buy your stock when no one wants it and sell it when everyone wants to buy.

This approach to investing is just another way of saying "buy low and sell high." A stock's price is determined by supply and demand. That is, if more people want to buy a stock than there are shares available from people who want to sell, then the stock price will rise. Likewise, if more people want to sell the stock than there are buyers for it, the stock price will fall. If you invest contrary to the masses, you will buy your quality stock while there is little demand for it and the price is low. Then when other investors become interested in it and the price increases, you will sell it for a profit.

CHAPTER

14

Economics and the Stock Market

The U.S. economic condition is one of the more important factors affecting the direction in which the stock market will move. Perhaps the best example of this is the stock-market crash on October 19, 1987. On that day, the market closed down 508 points. That was the largest move in history and was a much greater plunge than Black Friday in 1929 that heralded the Great Depression. From the time the market closed on October 19 until it reopened on October 20, virtually every stock-market analyst and economist predicted how bad the market would be on the 20th. Many anticipated that the crash would bring on a depression as Black Friday did. They were wrong. The U.S. economy was strong and instead of the stock-market crash affecting the economy, the economy affected the stock market. On October 20, the market experienced a 103-point rally, which was the second largest stock movement in history.

Throughout November and December, the fallout continued as the "doom-and-gloom" market analysts speculated that retailers were going to be badly hurt by the crash. Predictions were running the gamut from a slight recession to a full-blown depression. I disagreed with those analysts. The economic statistics just weren't that bad; in fact, they were pretty good. As the months passed, it became apparent that there wouldn't be a depression, not even a recession. Even the Dow rebounded to its precrash record highs and surpassed them, breaking 3,000 in June of 1990.

Figure 14.1   Gross National Product

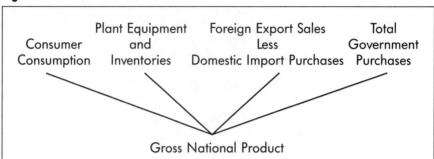

Why was *The CHEAP Investor* right and so many analysts with all their computers, charts and expensive equipment wrong? Most analysts were evidently assuming that the market would affect the economy. However, I believed that economic indicators demonstrated an economy that was strong enough to weather the crash.

To understand how the market moves, you must first understand what moves the market. I believe that the economic indicators, key statistics showing the direction of the economy, can be used to loosely predict market trends. Among the indicators are the Gross National Product (GNP), the Consumer Price Index (CPI), the Producer Price Index (PPI), interest rates, inflation and the unemployment rate.

I am not surprised that historical comparisons of stock indexes and the measures of economic activity, such as the GNP, CPI and PPI and the interest and unemployment rates, indicate a correlation between the direction of stock prices and the general state of the economy.

This chapter will explain each of the major economic indicators, show how they have performed over the past several years and demonstrate what effect the indicators have on the economy in general and on the stock market in particular.

THE GROSS NATIONAL PRODUCT (GNP)

The GNP measures the activity and market prices of all goods and services produced during the year. It is the value of goods and services bought and sold, including consumer consumption, investment in business equipment, foreign investment in the United States and government purchases (see Figure 14.1). The GNP growth rate is the primary indicator of the status of the economy. Figures on the GNP are released every quarter.

Figure 14.2 Real Gross National Product

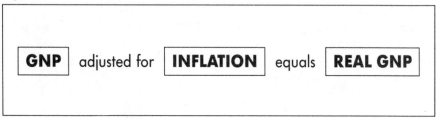

| GNP | adjusted for | INFLATION | equals | REAL GNP |

There are two basic ways to measure the Gross National Product. The first is the flow-of-income approach. Households provide business firms with resources (labor, entrepreneurial ability, property, etc.). For those resources, businesses pay rent, wages and salaries, interest and profits to members of the households. If all the resource payments were added up, they would make up the national income. Combining indirect taxes collected by the government (mostly property and sales taxes) and depreciation allowances (found on business firms' tax returns) with the national income creates the Gross National Product.

Another method of measuring the GNP uses expenditures, adding all the money spent by individual consumers, business firms and the government. For example, consumers receive income from businesses in return for their labor, property, etc. Then the money the consumers received flows back to various firms in exchange for goods and services. The money circulates as more goods are produced and paid for and more individuals are hired to produce the goods. If business-investment expenditures and government expenditures are added to the consumer expenditures previously described, the total is the GNP.

Comparing the GNP from one year to the next can be misleading. If, for example, the GNP increased from $4 trillion to $4.4 trillion, it would appear the GNP has done quite well, increasing by ten percent. However, before we celebrate, we must remember that the GNP measured all the goods and services produced that year *at market prices.* If, because of inflation, prices rose ten percent that year, we actually are just breaking even. Because inflated prices can make the GNP rise while actual production has remained the same, the *real GNP* has been devised to take inflation into account and give a more accurate picture of our growth (see Figure 14.2).

The GNP is extremely important for it reveals the condition of our economic system. Table 14.1 shows our real GNP changes for the past several years.

The GNP indicates the direction in which the country is headed. The optimum growth percentage is between 2.5 and 3.5 percent. Once

Table 14.1   Real Gross National Product Since 1982

Year	Percent	Year	Percent
1982	–2.5	1986	2.8
1983	3.6	1987	3.4
1984	6.8	1988	3.8
1985	3.4	1989	2.5
		1990	1.8

the economy starts growing more than four percent, it may become inflationary, causing interest rates to rise and that can be disastrous to the stock market.

The GNP is used to determine when the country is economically healthy. For example, a recession has been defined as two consecutive quarters of negative growth in the GNP. Interestingly, from mid-1990 through the beginning of 1991, the vast majority of analysts and economists referred to the U.S. economy as being in a recession. While several industries certainly experienced a big downturn, the U.S. economy had not actually met the classic criteria for a true recession.

THE CONSUMER PRICE INDEX (CPI)

The CPI measures change in consumer prices determined from a monthly survey tabulated by the U.S. Bureau of Labor Statistics. The survey is designed to compare price changes in goods and services over a period of time and is based on a sample of prices in seven major categories—food and beverages, housing, clothing and personal items, transportation, medical care, entertainment and energy.

The Consumer Price Index also is known as the Cost-of-Living Index, which is important to millions of people who receive cost-of-living pay increases. That group includes more than 40 million Social-Security beneficiaries, almost four million retired military and Federal government employees, more than 20 million food-stamp recipients and more than ten million workers covered by collective-bargaining agreements.

Ever since 1974 when the CPI hit double digits, there has been wide interest by the media, financial community, unions, employees and retirees who want to know whether they are keeping up or falling behind when comparing what we earn with what we have to spend. The Bureau

Table 14.2 Consumer Price Index Yearly Changes from 1967

Year	Percent	Year	Percent	Year	Percent
1967	2.9	1975	9.1	1983	3.2
1968	4.2	1976	5.8	1984	4.3
1969	5.4	1977	6.5	1985	3.6
1970	5.9	1978	7.7	1986	1.9
1971	4.3	1979	13.3	1987	3.6
1972	3.3	1980	13.5	1988	4.4
1973	6.2	1981	10.3	1989	4.8
1974	11.0	1982	6.2	1990	6.2

chose 1967 as the CPI's base year and assigned it an index number of 100. Prices for other years are reported from this base.

Example: In 1990, it took $385.37 to purchase the same $100 of goods and services in 1967.

Each month, the Bureau of Labor Statistics buys a fixed "market basket" of goods and services from the seven categories. To reflect changes in consumer spending, the "market basket," which determines the CPI, is revised every few years. Table 14.2 shows the major yearly changes in the CPI.

The high percentage jumps in the CPI in 1974, 1975, 1979, 1980, 1981 and 1990 were caused by dramatically increased oil prices. High oil prices had profound consequences on financial markets worldwide.

The Consumer Price Index reflects the inflation rate. It is very significant to the financial markets because if prices increase by a high rate, it raises the amount of money the government must pay to accomplish its job, which increases the budget deficit. If the budget deficit expands too fast, it has a disastrous effect on the financial markets and could cause them to crash. Over the years, analysts have found that a CPI of 3 to 4.5 percent sustains our economic health. A figure of more than 6 percent generally is considered inflationary.

THE PRODUCER PRICE INDEX (PPI)

Formerly called the Wholesale Price Index, the PPI measures changes in the wholesale prices of products and services. It is calculated and

Table 14.3 Producer Price Index Yearly Changes from 1967

Year	Percent	Year	Percent	Year	Percent
1967	1.0	1975	9.3	1983	.6
1968	2.8	1976	4.6	1984	1.7
1969	4.8	1977	6.1	1985	1.8
1970	2.2	1978	7.8	1986	−2.3
1971	4.0	1979	12.6	1987	2.2
1972	6.5	1980	11.8	1988	3.3
1973	13.1	1981	7.1	1989	4.9
1974	18.9	1982	3.6	1990	5.6

released on a monthly basis by the Bureau of Labor Statistics. Prices are measured as products move through the manufacturing and distribution stages of our economy to the consumer. The index is broken down into the components of commodity, industry, sector and stage of processing. Table 14.3 indicates the PPI changes from 1967 to 1990.

The Producer Price Index is probably the most accurate reflection of the change in wholesale inflation. Table 14.3 shows a dramatic reduction in the PPI changes since 1981.

If the Producer Price Index increases, usually six or eight months later those higher prices are reflected as a higher rate in the Consumer Price Index. Therefore, if the PPI increases by 6 or 7 percent, it may show up several months later as an 8- to 9-percent increase on the CPI.

THE INTEREST RATE

Interest rates fluctuate according to the laws of supply and demand. As the demand for money increases, interest rates rise. As the rates rise, the price of borrowing money becomes too high and the demand for money declines. When less money is borrowed, the supply of available money expands and interest rates fall as the supply of funds exceeds the demand for funds at the current rates.

At lower interest rates, business firms borrow more for investment purposes (such as building a new facility or expanding into a new market). Why? Because at a very high interest rate, few investment projects are worthwhile. However, as the interest rate declines, more and more investment projects become feasible.

Two major indicators show the direction of interest rates—the discount rate and the prime rate. The discount rate is the rate of interest

Table 14.4 Discount Rate Since 1970

Year	High	Low	Year	High	Low	Year	High	Low
1970	6.0	5.5	1977	6.0	5.25	1984	9.0	8.0
1971	5.0	4.5	1978	9.5	6.0	1985	8.0	7.5
1972	4.5	4.5	1979	12.0	9.5	1986	7.5	5.5
1973	7.5	4.5	1980	13.0	10.0	1987	6.0	5.5
1974	8.0	7.75	1981	14.0	12.0	1988	6.5	6.0
1975	7.8	6.0	1982	12.0	8.5	1989	7.0	7.0
1976	6.0	5.25	1983	8.5	8.5	1990	7.0	6.5

charged by the central bank of the Federal Reserve System to member banks who borrow and pledge securities or other assets for collateral (see Table 14.4). The discount rate also provides a floor for interest rates. Member banks would not charge customers an interest rate below the discount rate for that is the interest rate the member bank has to pay.

As the discount rate is either raised or lowered, it influences the prime rate, which is the lowest interest rate a commercial bank will charge its preferred customers for short-term, unsecured debts (see Table 14.5). The discount and prime rates are significant to the consumer, business and government because they will determine the direction in which general interest rates will move. Any time the prime rate or discount rate is adjusted, it is reported in the business section of newspapers across the country.

Interest rates are regulated by the Federal Reserve Board, a government agency that controls the amount of money that flows through our economic system. It is the Federal Reserve Board's responsibility to set the trends of interest rates by adjusting the discount rate.

Table 14.5 Prime Rate Since 1970

Year	High	Low	Year	High	Low	Year	High	Low
1970	8.5	6.75	1977	7.75	6.25	1984	13.0	10.75
1971	6.75	5.25	1978	11.75	7.75	1985	10.75	9.5
1972	6.0	5.0	1979	15.75	11.5	1986	9.0	7.5
1973	10.0	6.0	1980	21.5	10.75	1987	9.75	8.0
1974	12.0	9.75	1981	20.5	15.75	1988	10.5	8.5
1975	10.5	7.0	1982	17.0	11.5	1989	11.0	10.0
1976	7.25	6.25	1983	11.5	10.5	1990	10.0	10.0

When the Federal Reserve Board raises the discount rate, its member banks, in turn, raise their interest rates since it now costs them more to borrow. On the other hand, if the Federal Reserve Board lowers the discount rate, its member banks usually lower their interest rates accordingly.

The Federal Reserve Board also determines reserve requirements for banks, which changes the amount of money a bank can lend. By loosening or tightening the supply of money a bank can lend, the board can help regulate the economy. In addition, the Federal Reserve Board directly controls margin requirements, which affect both large and small investors.

Interest rates are extremely important to the economy. Just about everyone borrows money. The rates affect the consumer in the form of mortgages, automobile and personal loans, credit-card finance charges and home-equity loans. Both small and large businesses must borrow money for expansion, inventory financing, day-to-day expenses and many other reasons. The government borrows to continue serving U.S. citizens through a multitude of programs. The Federal Reserve Board walks a tightrope between allowing too much borrowing, which becomes inflationary, and not permitting enough borrowing, which could cause a recession as consumers and businesses reduce spending, which, in turn, spirals into further spending cuts.

There is a tremendous conflict of opinion on interest rates. I personally believe that if you note any major long-term trend in interest rates, the opposite trend will affect the stock market. For example, those who guessed or predicted that interest rates would drop drastically from a high prime rate of 20.5 percent in 1981 to about half that rate in four years could also have predicted that the stock market would soar.

In general, if you compare the longer-term trends in interest-rate movements and the stock market, you will observe a correlation between the two. Normally, if interest rates move up, the stock market will move down and vice versa. However, when interest rates are adjusted just a half a point up or down, this probably will not have much influence on the market. Another viewpoint is that when the prime rate fluctuates between 7 and 11 percent, companies and investors usually are interested in borrowing money. However, once the prime rate hits 12 percent or higher, they hesitate to borrow, which slows expansion and investment.

INFLATION

Like death and taxes, inflation seems to be unavoidable. In many cases, it is self-perpetuating. As consumers see prices rising and reasonably assume that prices will continue to do so, they rush out to buy more goods and services before prices climb even higher. When businesses see that by increasing prices they actually help their sales, they are encouraged to continue the trend by raising prices again.

Inflation can be caused by several different situations. When there is more demand for goods and services than can be produced, prices will increase. Because wages constitute the majority of the cost of doing business, any significant wage increase must be passed along to consumers in the form of higher prices. These increased prices raise everyone's cost of living, creating a demand for further wage increases.

Many industries are controlled by a few dominant companies that are so powerful that they can dictate prices in that industry, causing rising prices. Inflation also can be caused by supply-side cost shocks. The extreme increases in oil prices in 1973 and 1979 are good examples of this type of inflation. In 1990, oil prices soared from $17 per barrel in July to more than $40 in September due to concerns about oil shortages caused by the August Iraqi invasion and occupation of Kuwait. In this case, there was no shortage; in fact, there was an oversupply of oil. Therefore, once the panic subsided, oil prices and the inflation rate dropped dramatically in October, November and December.

The inflation rates are reflected by the Consumer Price Index as shown in Figure 14.3. While virtually no one would be alarmed by a one or two percent annual increase in the CPI, anything above six percent is considered hyperinflation. During a hyperinflationary trend, it becomes increasingly difficult to conduct normal economic activities. Prices constantly climb and it becomes almost impossible to enter into long-term contracts.

Inflation and interest rates go hand in hand. Because of the regulation by the Federal Reserve Board, if inflation rises too fast, interest rates will be raised to restrain the inflationary trend.

As interest rates rise, the cost of doing business increases, causing even higher inflation, which negatively affects the stock market. As inflation is regulated by higher interest rates and eventually starts to move downward, it positively impacts the stock market.

THE UNEMPLOYMENT RATE

The Bureau of Labor Statistics conducts a random survey of 60,000 households to compute the unemployment rate. The survey asks three questions:

Figure 14.3 Monthly Inflation Change

1. Are you working?
2. Did you work at all this month—even for one day?
3. Did you look for work during the month?

If an individual answers "yes" to questions 1 or 2, he or she is classified as employed. If the individual answers "yes" only to question 3, he or she is considered unemployed. However, if the individual answered "no" to all three questions, he or she is labeled a "discouraged worker" and does not get counted as unemployed. Table 14.6 shows the unemployment rate for the past several years.

It is important to follow the unemployment statistics because they can also affect how the stock market moves. Double-digit unemployment is considered negative for the stock market because a large percentage of potential consumers will be restricting their purchases, causing business to slow down. On the other hand, unemployment under 3.5 percent is also negative because it can create a demand greater than the supply of products, which may cause businesses to raise their prices as they pay higher wages to attract more employees to manufacture additional

Table 14.6 Unemployment Rate from 1980

Year	Percent	Year	Percent	Year	Percent
1980	7.1	1984	7.5	1988	5.5
1981	7.6	1985	7.2	1989	5.6
1982	9.7	1986	7.0	1990	5.8
1983	9.6	1987	6.2		

products. An unemployment rate between five and seven percent is usually considered good for inflation, interest rates and the market.

While I have gone into great detail explaining some of the prime economic indicators, you don't have to spend hours studying them each month when they are released. A good habit to form, however, would be to glance through the Sunday newspaper's business section each week looking for the release of any indicators and then ascertaining if there is any upward or downward trend. (A trend would be an upward or downward movement that has continued for at least three or four months.)

Once you have pinpointed a trend, you can take it into consideration when reviewing your portfolio. If you have followed my advice in choosing quality, low-priced stocks, your main concern would be whether or not to take a profit in your investments if you detect a trend that could have a negative impact on the stock market.

CHAPTER

$$\boxed{15}$$

Profiting from Volatility

At one time, an investor could purchase a quality stock, put it in a safe-deposit box and forget about it while it grew over the years into a nice nest egg for retirement. Unfortunately, that is not true today. Technology has changed the playing rules of investments. Instead of putting your stock away and letting it grow, today's money is made by actively trading stocks. The vast majority of stocks are cyclical and smart investors can make much more by purchasing a stock near its 52-week low and selling near its high than by holding it for long-term appreciation.

Up-to-the-minute information about stock prices, markets and indexes is readily available to everyone. In Chicago, three TV channels broadcast major investment programs during the hours the market is open. While the programs broadcast news on the latest developments that could affect the market or interview various individuals, the NYSE and ASE trades are listed at the bottom of the TV screen. In addition, the investor can receive the latest stock-trade prices on a home computer over the telephone line or from a satellite dish or FM receiver.

Computers have revolutionized the stock market. Orders to buy and sell stocks, bonds, mutual funds, etc., are transmitted around the world at the speed of light. Computers provide instant confirmation of trades, up-to-the-second quotes for stocks and diverse information that normally would not be easily accessible for the small investor. Not only is computerized information a tremendous asset for the small investor, it is vital to institutions, large brokerage firms and portfolio managers.

Computerized program trading has been spawned by the modern age of high-speed communications and computerized stock trading. Because the trader can react so quickly to market changes, program trading is an invaluable tool that is used and abused. For better or worse, it has totally changed the marketplace, causing tremendous market volatility in a short period of time. Program trading was a major culprit behind the stock market crash of 1987.

A small investor can make huge profits by not panicking when the market is extremely volatile and taking advantage of swings that cause stock prices to plunge to unrealistic lows. Buying quality stocks that are undervalued can prove extremely profitable.

VOLATILITY — A LEGACY OF THE CRASH OF 1987

I have referred to the 1987 stock market crash several times in this book because we still are feeling repercussions from it today. Stock market volatility became a major issue because of the crash and restrictions on the amount of upward or downward swings have been put into place to avoid plunges such as the one we experienced then.

On October 19, 1987, the stock market, as measured by the Dow Jones Industrials, experienced the largest single-day movement in its history. Unfortunately, the movement was down — 508 points or about 22 percent. This disastrous plunge caused widespread panic. Stock-market analysts and economic experts predicted a great depression or at least a major recession for 1988. This didn't happen.

What caused the crash of 1987? The day after the 508-point plunge, I wrote an editorial for *The CHEAP Investor* that explained, "We believe the blue-chip stocks were at record high prices because of *greed*. Most were way overpriced and then institutional buyers (who own a large percentage of blue chips) *panicked* and sold all day Monday (October 19th), causing a 22 percent drop in the Dow.

"By Tuesday, those embarrassed institutional buyers realized that the blue chips were now at an unrealistically low price and began buying them back." The editorial continued, "There is no doubt that what happened the week of October 19, 1987, will be remembered for the rest of our lives. Since investments are measured over a long period of time in peaks and valleys, hopefully we can look back at this valley as a great investment opportunity."

For the next couple of months after the crash, most of the "experts" were still predicting various forms of doom for our economy. They felt that the retailers would experience a very gloomy holiday season as most consumers would buy less-expensive gifts and entertain more economically. I disagreed. The economic indicators were all positive and while many investors had the breath punched out of them, I didn't think the crash was going to have that drastic an effect on the economy. The 1987 holiday season far exceeded the analysts' expectations.

The crash of 1987 created a lot of good buys...good-bye Jaguar... good-bye yacht...good-bye high life-style.... Seriously, it affected a lot of lives, but not so many and not as drastically as the analysts had predicted.

Events Leading to the Crash

To see the buildup of the crash potential, we'll go back in history to 1986 when it was the general consensus that we were experiencing the greatest bull market in our history. Wall Street analysts, institutions and individual investors started to buy virtually any stock or mutual fund at record high prices, assuming prices would continue to move higher. We saw 1986 close at 1,896. Practically every day, newspapers, magazines and TV newscasts headlined one broken Wall Street record after another. Everywhere you looked, you were bombarded with the wonderful news of how well the stock market was doing and how everyone was making lots of money. Needless to say, those who hadn't already invested wanted to join the crowd because they didn't want to miss out on a "sure thing."

On January 9, 1987, the market had skyrocketed through the 2,000 level and the media increased its coverage on the record-setting stock market. Foreign money was being invested in blue chips and mutual funds at record levels and the stock market continued its upward movement, closing the end of January at 2,163. Despite the continued upward record-setting movement, I started to see some signals of change. The trade deficit began to capture the media's attention as it hit a record monthly high on January 2, 1987, at $19.22 billion. Interest rates, inflation and other economic indicators hit bottom in 1986 and were showing signs of moving up. Oil prices hit an 11-month high, closing at $18 a barrel the first week in January, 1987. These indicators caused me to write an editorial in January of 1987 predicting a bullish 1987 for the first six months. I was concerned that the increasing oil prices, interest and inflation rates and deficit could come back to haunt us.

A big factor for the January, 1987, huge upward thrust in the market was a *Barron's* article quoting Robert Prechter, the self-proclaimed Wall Street guru. Prechter predicted that the Dow would hit 3,600 and the day the article was printed, the Dow claimed a new one-day jump record of 44 points. On January 22, the Dow soared 51 points. The excitement continued in February as the DOW shot up 54 points to 2,238 on the 17th due to foreign buying and something called program trading. February closed at 2,224.

In early March, Jim Wright, the Democratic Speaker of the House, announced that he was working toward a goal of raising taxes by about $20 billion a year. The Dow moved down in reaction to the announcement, but by the end of March was at 2,305. In April, interest rates started to move up, surprising Wall Street and inflicting large losses on bond debts of securities firms. The month closed down at 2,286. With the trade debt increasing, Congress tried to fix the problem with the Gephardt amendment, which called for major protectionist legislation. The financial markets shuddered at the prospect. The bill lost 218 to 214. The market closed at 2,297.

On June 3, Paul Volker resigned as chairman of the Federal Reserve Board and Alan Greenspan, a Volker clone, was nominated to take his place. Again the market shuddered and the dollar plunged. However, as the GNP indicators continued to increase, the dollar rebounded and the market started moving up again, closing in June at 2,418. In July, the major indicators continued to rise and *The Wall Street Journal* wrote that economic expansion would last at least another year. The market continued to soar then ticked downward when legislation was passed by the Senate calling for action against countries with a "consistent pattern of import barriers" (Japan). By mid-July, strong foreign buying and computerized program trading moved the market upward so July closed at 2,572.

In the beginning of August, oil prices began to tumble, sparking a rally in the stock market. On August 11th, the market broke 2,600 and two days later it was at 2,680. As the media blitz about the amazing market grew, individuals who didn't want to miss "the opportunity to make money" bought just about anything at record-high prices. On August 25th, the market hit an all-time high of 2,746.65 but closed at 2,722.42. IBM hit a high of 174 and fell as analysts reduced the company's 1987 earnings estimates. Other major stocks followed the downward movement. The trade deficit widened to a new record of $39.53 billion in the second quarter, causing the market to continue its fall. August closed at 2,662.95.

Early in September, oil prices moved up to near $20 and on September 3, the Federal Reserve Board raised the discount rate from 5.5

percent to 6.5 percent. The prime rate rose from 8.25 percent to 8.75 percent. The dollar plunged, causing the stock market to fall to 2,549 by September 9. Several major analysts, including Stan Weinstein of the *Professional Tape Reader*, concluded that 2,549 would be the low point. Prechter continued to be bullish, never losing faith that the Dow would hit 3,600 before the next bear market. The market seesawed, closing at 2,596 in September.

By October 13, the market was down to 2,508. The next day, Prechter had a change of heart and revised his outlook to include a 300-point drop in the Dow before it rose to 3,600. The Dow plunged 91 points. Congress was having trouble meeting the Gramm-Rudman budget reduction targets and put a $12-billion-tax package together. Troubles continued with the trade deficit and the value of the dollar. An American-registered tanker was hit in Kuwaiti waters, causing oil prices to soar. These all contributed to the 260-point drop between October 14 and 16. When the market closed Friday, October 16 it stood at 2,246, primarily because of mass selling by institutional buyers through portfolio selling and computerized sell programs.

Program trading accounted for a stunning 43 percent of the NYSE total volume. During the last half hour, the selling hysteria reached such a magnitude that it was destined to continue on Monday. Instead of being a cooling-off period, the weekend of October 17 and 18 intensified the bearish attitude.

The Day of the Crash

On October 19, the stock market experienced its now famous plunge. Friday's needless computer-driven program trading by institutions would continue with force that Monday. What may have been prudent selling on Friday had turned into wholesale desertion over the weekend.

The year 1987 was the year of the mutual fund as institutional and individual investors bought mutual funds at record-high prices, assuming they would continue to move upward. The Fidelity group of mutual funds was considered king and when Fidelity bought a stock, Wall Street would follow. One of the big sellers on the morning of October 19 would be Fidelity offering to sell more than $1 billion in assets and of course, everyone followed.

As the day began, overseas markets plunged: London down 22 percent; Tokyo down 17 percent; Zurich down 14 percent; Frankfurt down 13 percent; Hong Kong down 11 percent; Singapore down 33 percent. More bad news hit the wires at 7 AM EST when it was announced that two Iranian oil platforms had been leveled by the United States. This seemed to fuel the mass selling orders of foreign and institutional investors.

To address the situation before the opening of the New York Stock Exchange, John Phelan, its chairman, said, "The way to make sure stocks open well in volatile markets is don't open them quickly." This backfired and caused more panic selling. In fact, the later a stock opened, the lower was its opening price.

Figure 15.1 shows the Friday closing prices of the 30 Dow Industrial stocks and their opening prices on Monday morning. Every stock opened lower than it closed on Friday and most continued to fall during the day because of the herd instinct and the computerized selling of institutions.

When the market opened at 9:30 AM EST, the stock index futures plunged, causing the Dow to drop 50 points almost immediately (see Figure 15.2). In addition, the delay in opening hundreds of stocks caused more anxiety and worsened the situation. The selling pressure was so severe that by 11 AM all but one of the Dow 30 stocks had opened and the Dow had moved down more than 200 points to 2,025. In a correction, the market moved up slightly to 2,125 by 12 noon.

However, major margin calls for takeover stocks caused the market to move back down to 2,050 by 1 PM. With rumors abounding that the SEC and the exchanges were considering closing the markets, the Dow continued down to about 1,975 by 2 PM. A small correction showed 2,000 at 2:45 PM and then panic reigned. Headed by computerized sell programs, institutions, mutual funds, foreign and individual sellers started to sell at any price. They got their wish and the market plunged from 2,000 to 1,738. The only thing that stopped the hysterical selling was the closing bell.

The result was the worst loss experienced by the stock market in 78 years. The Dow had dropped an incredible 508 points in 6½ hours. This was a day that everyone will remember for the rest of our lives. We'll tell our children and grandchildren about October 19th just as our grandfathers told us about Black Friday in 1929.

The Next Day — A Recovery

On Tuesday, the 20th, the overseas markets were relatively calm despite the fact that several markets were down including Tokyo, which fell 225 points or about 9 percent, London which dropped 13 percent and

Figure 15.1   Dow Jones Industrials Stock Change, October 19, 1987

Close 10-16-87	Company Name	Open 10-19-87	Close 10-19-87	Points Down
56.00	Alcoa	51.00	42.50	13.50
39.13	Allied Signal	35.50	27.63	11.50
30.00	AT&T	28.38	23.63	6.38
16.50	Bethlehem Steel	15.75	11.00	5.50
43.63	Boeing	41.88	38.50	5.13
49.50	Chevron	47.50	41.25	8.25
40.50	Coca Cola	36.25	30.50	10.00
98.50	DuPont	90.00	80.50	18.00
43.75	Exxon	40.00	33.50	10.25
50.75	General Electric	42.00	41.88	8.88
66.00	General Motors	65.38	60.00	6.00
59.50	Goodyear Tire	53.00	42.50	17.00
135.00	IBM	122.00	103.25	31.75
46.38	International Paper	41.00	33.88	12.50
90.13	Kodak	75.63	62.88	27.25
43.63	McDonalds	40.50	36.38	7.25
184.00	Merek	162.00	160.00	24.00
70.25	Minnesota Mining	64.00	56.00	14.25
6.00	Navistar International	5.88	4.88	1.13
102.75	Philip Morris	90.00	88.13	14.63
44.38	Primerica	41.38	34.13	10.25
85.00	Proctor & Gamble	82.00	61.38	23.63
41.50	Sears Roebuck	36.75	31.00	10.50
36.50	Texaco	32.00	32.00	4.50
27.38	Union Carbide	26.25	24.75	2.63
48.63	United Tech.	46.50	41.00	7.63
34.00	USX Corp.	32.25	21.50	12.50
60.50	Westinghouse	51.00	40.25	20.25
42.50	Woolworth	41.25	36.50	6.00

Frankfurt, which declined 5 percent. Before the market opened on Tuesday, Alan Greenspan, Federal Reserve Board chairman, stated, "The Federal Reserve affirms its readiness to serve as a source of liquidity to support the economic and financial system." This support was probably a major reason why there were a vast number of buy orders by institutions when the market opened and those orders helped precipitate the market

Figure 15.2 The October 19, 1987, Crash

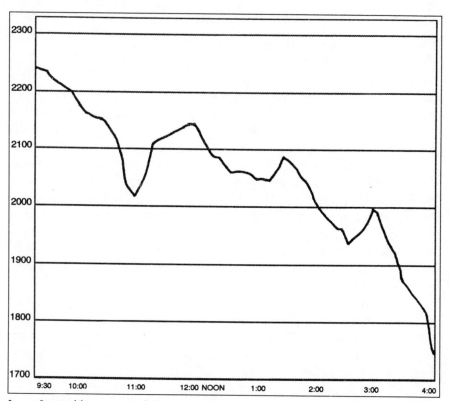

rally. On the 20th, the market soared, hitting a high of 2,067 or + 325 points, but closed at 1,841 up 103 points.

It was mainly the higher-priced and blue-chip stocks that suffered major losses on October 19; however, October 20 was more disastrous to the small investor. As the media created a Super Bowl atmosphere about the stock-market crash, the small investor understandably became more anxious and confused. The 20th saw an influx of sell orders from small investors in lower-priced stocks. In some cases, a vicious cycle was created as the mass selling caused margin calls that made the stock price decline further, causing more panic selling and margin calls.

With hindsight, it is easy to look back to see the signs indicating that the bull market we experienced couldn't go on much longer. Using common sense and the economic indicators, you can determine your own investing strategy to take those factors into consideration.

VOLATILITY CAUSED BY THE
MIDDLE EAST OIL CRISIS

During mid- to late-1990, investors had the opportunity to profit during the huge drop in the Dow Jones Industrials from 3,034 in June to 2,350 in October. The crisis was caused by Saddam Hussein and his Iraqi army that invaded Kuwait on August 2, 1990. The invasion precipitated an almost 700-point drop occurring over a three-month period as oil prices at the pump were going up. Figure 15.3 shows the 700-point decline.

That 700-point drop was far more devastating than the 500-point drop in 1987 because it was a long-term decline unlike the 1987 plunge that showed good recovery the next day. The combination of continually falling stock prices and rising gasoline prices crushed investor confidence and kept many from investing in potentially lucrative undervalued stocks. According to the Consumer Confidence Index, which hit a high of 82 percent in June, consumer confidence fell to a low of 68 percent at the end of 1990.

The panic resulting from the crisis caused many quality stock prices to plunge to the point where they were very undervalued. Investors who follow the Contrarian philosophy realize that this is a great opportunity. It just takes a certain amount of courage to buy your bargain stock when everyone else is selling.

WAYS TO PROFIT FROM VOLATILITY

While major market plunges can create many bargains, volatility in an industry can also affect stock prices. For example, companies that mine gold, silver or platinum usually see their stocks move upward or downward in response to increasing or decreasing prices of their particular metals.

I like to follow oil commodity prices because many oil stocks are also affected by fluctuations in the price per barrel of oil. For example, in May of 1988, the commodity price dropped to $15 per barrel and oil stocks in general were near their 52-week low prices. I recommended Galveston-Houston at $1.75 per share. Listed on the NYSE, it had experienced hard times, but had started to turn its balance sheet around. Over the next year, as the price of crude oil increased, Galveston-Houston's stock soared to more than $7 or +300 percent! Because the price per barrel was still near $15 in August of 1988, I recommended

Figure 15.3 Dow Jones Industrials Plunge During Middle East Oil Crisis

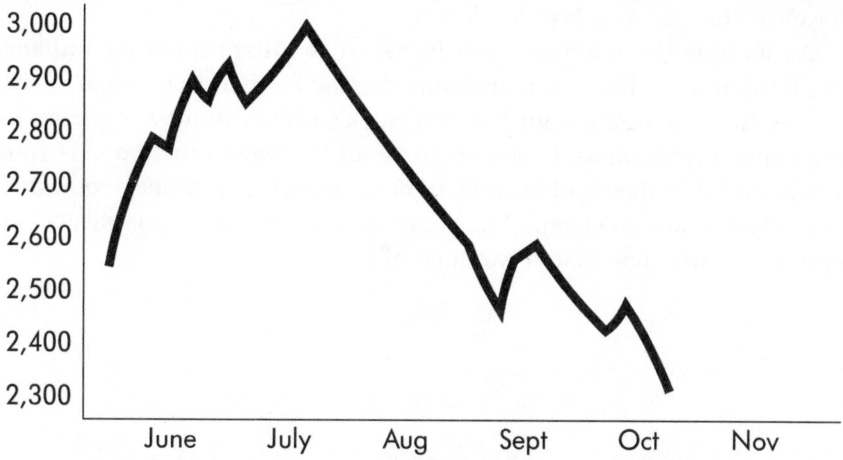

Source: Reprinted by permission of *Barron's*, ©1991 Dow Jones & Company, Inc. All Rights Reserved Worldwide.

Varco International listed on the NYSE at $3. Its price has since skyrocketed to $13.75 or +358 percent.

However, when oil prices fell in the summer of 1990 to $17 per barrel, the situation was different because many oil companies' stocks were near the high points of their cycles. For example, Galveston-Houston's price was more than $6 and Varco was at $12. When crude oil prices shot up from $17 to more than $40, there were many headlines about the huge profits that were made in oil stocks. Unfortunately, the headlines were misleading because the individuals who wrote those articles assumed that most oil stocks soared as oil commodity prices rose. That didn't happen this time. Those writers didn't realize that two conditions are necessary for oil stock prices to jump when oil commodity prices shoot up. Not only should the price per barrel be low, but the quality oil companies' stocks should be near their 52-week low price. The best way to ensure a profit is to find a stock that meets both requirements.

When volatility causes stocks in a certain industry to fall, don't be so overwhelmed by "bargains" that you forget to completely analyze the company. Make sure it meets the normal requirements of price—near the 52-week low, with good sales and good earnings.

The trend toward volatility has scared many investors. If you want to be a successful investor, instead of following the herd, be a Contrarian. Perhaps one of the hardest lessons to learn is that when stock prices plunge due to volatility in an industry or the stock market as a whole, this creates some fantastic bargains. A certain amount of courage is needed to think positively when almost everyone else is crying the blues. However, this can pay big dividends.

As long as the company you invest in is a high-quality company, even if the market has fallen and may decline further, the company will survive. At some point, your bargain stock's price will move up from its undervalued position and you can smile all the way to the bank as your friends wish that they had been farsighted enough to purchase so-and-so stock when it was so cheap. The smart investor looks at volatility as an opportunity that few take advantage of.

CHAPTER

16

The Scamproof Investor

After the 1987 crash, thousands of small investors have hesitated to purchase stocks. Many were cash rich and ripe for picking by scam artists. According to the North American Securities Administrators Association, in 1988 alone, investors were bilked out of more than $250 million in gold swindles. Gold swindles aren't the only scams being pulled. Those high-pressure artists will gladly take your money in oil wells, commodities, futures, options and penny stocks.

☐   **RULE 11**   ☐

Don't take anyone else's word; investigate before you invest.

INVESTIGATE BEFORE YOU INVEST

When an investor talks to his or her broker or salesperson, many times the investor becomes so concerned about how much money can be made that he or she forgets to ask any questions about the investment. Letting someone else make your investment decisions for you is certainly easier than taking the responsibility yourself; however, this makes you more susceptible to high-pressure investment scam artists.

Let's look at some investment scams to help you recognize the different aspects involved. Of course, one ingredient that is always there is the investor's greed—a greed so great that it blinds the investor to the scam.

Classic Commodity
Half-and-Half Scam

This scam has been used by aggressive brokers who pick any volatile commodity such as September pork bellies. Starting with a list of perhaps 500 prospective investors, the broker will call half of the investors and tell them to buy. The other half will be told to sell. Needless to say, 250 investors will be impressed with the broker's advice because the pork bellies will either have moved up or down as "predicted."

Then the broker will contact the 250 people who were correctly advised and again divide the group in half, advising 125 to buy and 125 to sell another volatile commodity. Once that commodity either goes up or down, the broker contacts the group that has been twice correctly advised. That group of potential investors by now is extremely impressed with this financial wizard and many will blindly follow his or her "superior" investment advice. This tactic provides the commodity broker with a steady stream of customers and commissions. The same scam can be adapted by brokers in futures, options and stocks.

How do you protect yourself from such a scam? One way is to investigate the broker before you trust him or her with thousands of your dollars. You can contact your state securities commissioner or local Better Business Bureau to verify that the broker and his or her firm are duly licensed in your state and to learn whether either has been disciplined by any regulatory agency. If the broker has been using underhanded methods to sell securities previously, there's a chance that complaints have been lodged against him or her. You can contact the following associations:

U.S. brokers or brokerage firms:
National Association of Securities Dealers (NASD)
9513 Key West Avenue
Rockville, MD 20850-3389
301-590-6500
(A NASD office is located in each state, usually in the capital. You can call directory assistance for the local NASD office.)

Canadian brokers, brokerage firms or companies:
Office of Superintendent of Financial Institutions
255 Albert Street
Ottawa, Ontario K1A 0H2
613-990-7788

Commodity or futures brokers or brokerage firms:
Commodity Futures Trading Commission (CFTC)
2033 K Street N.W.
Washington, DC 20581
202-254-8630

Following are nine tips that investors will want to observe when considering an investment. Because purchasing stock may involve a lot of money, it can be an expensive lesson if you make a mistake. While the vast majority of brokers and financial analysts are honest, you should be aware that there are unethical salespeople. Misrepresentation of a stock's value and outright fraud do occur.

Scamproofing Your Investments

1. Never buy investments offered over the telephone; always ask for information about the investments in writing so you can review it.
2. Beware of the broker who applies high pressure for you to buy immediately.
3. Check the references of any broker you don't know who tries to sell an investment to you.
4. Be suspicious of "guarantees" of quick or huge profits.
5. Never buy on tips or rumors. It is more prudent to get all the facts first. Besides, it is illegal to buy or sell stock based on "inside information."
6. Recognize the fact that in an investment program, success in the past is no guarantee of success in the future.
7. If you don't understand something in a prospectus or a sales brochure, get advice.
8. Don't speculate unnecessarily. While speculation can be a worthwhile investment tool for knowledgeable, experienced investors who understand the risks involved, for the average investor, speculation is too risky.
9. Be extremely careful with tax-sheltered investments and limited partnerships or any other investment that claims a much higher return than average.

SPOTTING AN INVESTMENT SCAM

Perhaps the best-known and most successful swindler of the 20th century was Charles A. Ponzi, who emigrated from Rome to the United States in 1903. He has the dubious distinction of being the father of the "Get Rich Quick" scheme. In 1919, Ponzi formed the Securities and Exchange Company (SEC) in Boston.

Ponzi's scam was simple—lend me your money for 45 days and I will pay back not only your principal but 50 percent interest. The gullible public flooded him with money—almost $10 million. He would pay back the early investors with new investors' money. This strategy worked until July, 1920 when Ponzi was bringing in more than $400,000 a day but couldn't repay earlier investors. Ponzi, the ultimate smooth talker, claimed, "The promise of a profit is not larceny, it is merely a promise, and a promise may or may not be kept according to the circumstances."

Almost 70 years after Charles Ponzi's company was shut down in 1920, the Ponzi scheme continues to flourish. Today's copycats create an aura of wealth with swanky offices, fine clothes and expensive cars (perhaps even a plane or helicopter). Potential investors are fed hints and suggestions about a "very profitable venture that is distributing extremely large profits to investors." Gullible and greedy investors still line up today to throw their money into such schemes.

It is ironic that the Securities Act of 1934 created the SEC (Securities and Exchange Commission) to regulate the securities industry. I sure hope it wasn't named in honor of Ponzi's famous company.

Today, there is a new emphasis on financial planning, which is one area that abounds with swindlers. According to a recent two-year study by a group of state securities examiners, fraud and abuse by financial planners caused 22,000 investors to lose nearly $400 million. The report concluded that "The rapid growth of the loosely regulated financial planning industry appears to have had the unintended side effect of paving the way for the swindlers and unscrupulous promoters who pose as financial planners." The study recommended that potential customers inquire about a planner's experience and professional background and request examples of his or her work and references.

One area with a tremendous number of scams and frauds is penny stocks, especially pink-sheet stocks. While a few investors get in on the ground floor of a legitimate company and sell the stock for a nice profit after its price rises, most investors are not that fortunate. Penny stocks are risky investments. A typical penny stock is poorly financed with an uncertain future. Because of its low price and relatively small number of shareholders, the stock can easily be manipulated by its underwriter or market maker.

Perhaps one of the most well-known examples is Bob Brennan of First Jersey Securities, who in his commercials used to step down from his helicopter and invite investors to "come grow with us." He would then promote the great investment opportunities in penny stocks. (You may have seen this ad a couple of years ago when it ran during the Super Bowl game.) After years of run-ins with the SEC on the quality of the penny stocks that his brokerage firm sold, Brennan was basically forced to leave the industry.

Another penny-stock scam was GoldCor, a Florida-based company that claimed to have a secret process for converting black volcanic beach sand in Costa Rica into gold. The secret process provided a great pitch (story) for penny-stock brokers to interest investors. A November, 1986, geologist report had concluded that GoldCor's gold-recovery process was a "scam and a fraud." However, the brokers and other GoldCor promoters ignored the report and claimed that the recovery process would be able to produce gold from the sand for more than 1,000 years.

The brokers used deceptive practices in promoting GoldCor, claiming that the stock posed no risk and that investors would receive a 200-percent profit within three months. The sad part is that many investors got blinded by their greed and believed them. Those brokers hyped the stock value from a couple hundred thousand dollars to almost $350 million in 1987.

The SEC filed suit against GoldCor, asserting that the operation was a fraud and charging that no gold had ever been refined using the company's equipment. GoldCor's stock, which was worth more than $350 million in 1987, is worth under $2 million ($ .01 per share) today.

An interesting scam was perpetrated by a teenager. Barry Minkow became a millionaire by promoting his carpet-cleaning company ZZZZ Best from nothing to a value of $100 million. (Now it is worth nothing again.) Investors were bilked out of more than $50 million. Many major brokerage firms were promoting the stock and it is hard to believe that no one checked ZZZZ Best's 10-K and 10-Q forms to discover that the firm actually had very little sales and assets. Worse yet, no one seems to have questioned why a small carpet-cleaning company with hardly any assets should be worth almost $100 million. Many of the people who lost their money foolishly bought the stock at record high prices, assuming that the stock would move higher.

You can find scams even in your mailbox. The other day I received an advertising cardek (a bundle of postcard-sized ads). Looking through it, I found some interesting statements on an advertisement (shown in Figure 16.1).

Let's review those statements. First of all, Apple Computer was never a penny stock for it went public for almost $20 per share. The statement is totally false. In the second example, you see typical penny-stock hype. If the firm resorts to such tactics in its advertising, what other tactics does it use to sell stocks? In the final example, Tandy and MCI were never penny stocks. The low price that is used in the example comes from the Standard & Poor's stock guide, which adjusts a stock's low price for stock splits. When a stock splits, say two for one, the low price, which may be $5, gets split also into $2.50. Over the years, the Standard & Poor's low price for companies such as Tandy and MCI, which have had several stock splits, has become quite small, even though the stock never sold at that price.

I learned a long time ago that determining which investments to avoid is a major step in deciding what to buy. Whenever you receive an unsolicited telephone call from a broker who wants to help you make money by investing in a great little company, beware. By asking two questions you can weed out many potential scams:

1. Where is the stock traded? If the salesperson says "the OTC market," ask where specifically. If it's either the pink sheets or the Vancouver Exchange, avoid the stock.
2. How did the company go public? If the company was a shell, a blind pool or a self-underwriting, stay away from the stock.

Figure 16.1 Deceptive Advertising

- Apple Computer. . . a penny stock? Not any more, but similar opportunities await the informed investor today. Don't miss the next opportunity!

- How to get rich—investing in the penny-stock market—while some investors have lost, find out how others have made fortunes in the penny-stock market.

- The most profitable penny stocks you never saw—MCI at $ .25 and Tandy (Radio Shack) at $ .63. These major companies were once penny stocks. . . .

REGULATION IN THE MARKET—THE SEC

Under the Federal securities laws, the major responsibility for regulating the conduct of the individuals and companies that buy and sell securities lies with self-regulatory organizations that are governed by the SEC. The self-regulatory organizations, such as the NASD, institute rules to supervise trading and other activities, establish qualifications for professionals in the securities industry, control the behavior of their members and discipline those members who ignore or break its rules.

The SEC's primary objectives are to make sure the securities markets operate in a fair and orderly manner, to assure the professionals in the securities industry deal honestly with their customers and to guarantee that corporations make public all the pertinent information an investor needs to make an intelligent investment decision.

The SEC serves as a watchdog to protect against fraud in the sale of securities, illegal sales practices, market manipulation and other violations of investors' trust by brokers and brokerage firms. The SEC can deny registration to securities firms and in some cases may impose sanctions against a firm and/or individual who violates the Federal securities laws. Abuses include misappropriation of customer funds or securities and manipulation of the market price of a stock.

Despite the many protections provided by federal and state securities laws, it is essential that investors know that they have the final responsibility for their own protection. In particular, the SEC can't guarantee the worth of any security. Each investor must make that judgment for himself or herself.

It is a good idea to check the SEC's library to see if any of the individuals connected with an investment have had sanctions imposed against them. There are several SEC offices located across the United States. The map in Figure 16.2 shows the regional and branch offices.

There are also some excellent publications that you may want to read:

What Every Investor Should Know
by the U.S. Securities and Exchange Commission
450 Fifth Street, N.W., Room 3C38
Washington, DC 20549
Telephone: 202-272-7460

Investment Swindles: How They Work and How To Avoid Them
by the National Futures Association
200 West Madison Street, Suite 1600
Chicago, Illinois 60606
Telephone: 800-621-3570 (800-572-9400 in Illinois)

Figure 16.2 SEC Offices in the United States

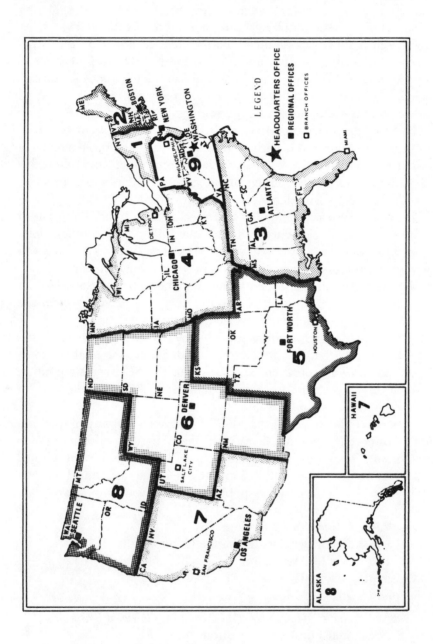

Source: *Q & A: Small Business and the SEC.*

Investor Alert—How To Protect your Money from Schemes, Scams, and Frauds
by the North American Securities Administration Association, Inc.
555 New Jersey Avenue, N.W., Suite 750
Washington, DC 20001
Telephone: 202-737-0900

The vast majority of all investment scams have one similarity—high-pressure telephone sales tactics. If you are offered a deal that's just too good to be true, it probably is. The best way of handling high-pressure, incredible telephone sales offers is to *hang up!*

CHAPTER

$$\boxed{17}$$

Investing Without Using Money

A painless way to test your expertise in buying and selling stocks is to simulate trading without actually investing the money. Simulation gives you the opportunity to gain experience in trading stocks. It allows you to learn from your mistakes without risk. In this chapter, you will apply the knowledge that you have learned from this book.

TYPICAL STOCK COMMISSION SCHEDULE

On pages 114 and 115, there are lists of both full-service and discount brokers. You can call or write several firms to request their commission schedule. When you read the schedules, you will probably notice variations in the commission fee depending on the trade dollar amount and the minimum commission charge. You can use that information to your advantage when purchasing a stock. If you already know what stock you want to buy, you might as well use the least-expensive brokerage firm.

To figure your total cost of buying and selling stocks, you need to include the brokerage firm's commission fee. The commission becomes an important element in the cost of investing when you realize that it directly affects your profits. It is easy to forget that fact when figuring profits. Many times, an investor will look at the price per share for both

Figure 17.1 Commission Schedule

Trade Dollar Amount	Commission Rates
$0 — $2,500	$ 25 + 1.6 percent of principal
2,501 — 6,000	$ 51 + .6 percent of principal
6,001 — 22,000	$ 69 + .3 percent of principal
22,001 — 50,000	$ 91 + .2 percent of principal
50,001 — 500,000	$141 + .1 percent of principal

buying and selling and figure that the difference is the profit. Unfortunately, if the investor buys only a few shares, it's very possible that his commission fees will consume the majority of that profit. I would recommend purchasing at least 1,000 shares if at all possible. The sample in Figure 17.1 shows how a typical commission schedule is set up.

With the schedule, you can determine your commission fee. For example, you want to buy 1,000 shares of Amrep Corporation at $3.75. Your stock price (principal) would be 1,000 multiplied by $3.75 or $3,750. Referring to the commission schedule, you see that $3,750 falls into the second category of $2,501—$6,000. The commission will be $51 plus $3,750 multiplied by .006 or $22.50. Your total commission is $51 plus $22.50 or $73.50. Adding that to your principal of $3,750 gives you a total purchase price of $3,823.50.

SIMULATING A STOCK TRADE

Any time you purchase a stock, you receive a confirmation from your brokerage firm that looks similar to the one in Figure 17.2.

The stock confirmation has ten areas of interest:

1. *You Bought/You Sold* tells how many shares were purchased if the amount is in the "You Bought" area or sold if in the "You Sold" area.
2. *Security Description* gives the name of the stock you traded.
3. *Price* is the cost per share for the stock.
4. *Trade Date* shows the date the stock was bought or sold.
5. *Settlement Date* specifies the date the payment is due at the brokerage firm if you bought or when the firm will issue a check to you if you sold.

Figure 17.2 Stock Confirmation

Stock Confirmation

In accordance with your instructions, the transaction below is confirmed for your account and risk subject to terms listed on the reverse side. Please refer to your account number when placing orders or making inquiries. Refer to the reverse side for instructions on endorsing and mailing certificates.

You Bought	You Sold	Security Description	Price	Trade Date	Settlement Date
1,000		Amrep Corporation	$3.75	2-15-91	2-22-91

Account Number	Gross Amount	Interest	Commission	Other	Net Amount
123456	$3,750.00		$73.50		$3,823.50

John Smith
1234 Fifth Street
New York, New York 10001

Confirmation—Customer's copy Retain for tax purposes.

---

6. *Account Number* is the number of your account with the brokerage firm.
7. *Gross Amount* is the price per share multiplied by the number of shares.
8. *Commission* shows the amount charged by the brokerage firm to either buy or sell the stock.
9. *Net Amount* is the total amount owed the brokerage firm if you bought or owed you if you sold.
10. *Name and Address* lists your name and address and should be checked for accuracy.

The stock confirmation indicates that on 2-15-91, you bought 1,000 shares of Amrep at $3.75 per share. The gross price is $3,750 plus $73.50 commission. Therefore, you owe the brokerage firm a total of $3,823.50, which is due at the firm on 2-22-91.

Figure 17.3 Company Information

Stock Record

Company Name *Amrep Corporation*

Address *16 West 61st St.*

City *New York*   State *NY*   Zip *10023*

Telephone Number *212-541-7300*

Exchange *NYSE* Stock Symbol *AXR*

52-Week High *8 3/8* 52-Week Low *3 1/4*

Stock Record Sheet

When you simulate a stock buy, you will want to include most of this information on your stock record. The blank form (Figure 17.8) at the end of the chapter will provide space for all the vital information for a particular stock investment on one easy-to-read page. The first section includes pertinent information on the company. If you were simulating the purchase of Amrep, it would be filled in as shown in Figure 17.3.

The Buy Transaction section contains all the important details of the stock purchase. At the bottom of the section, you should express your reasons for buying the stock and the price you project the stock will hit. It would look like Figure 17.4.

When you decide that it is time to sell your stock, you would complete the two bottom sections. The Sell Transaction records the money

Figure 17.4 Buy Transaction

Buy Transaction

Date *2-15-91*   Stock Price *$3,750.00*

Number of Shares *1,000* Plus Commission *73.50*

Price per Share *$3.75*   Purchase Price *3,823.50*

Why did you purchase the stock? *Good sales, good earnings. Low stock price near 52=week low*

Stock Price Projection *+50% in six to nine months*

you would receive when you sold the stock. You also want to write down your reason for selling the stock at that point. If you decided to sell Amrep at $6, this section would be completed as shown in Figure 17.5.

The final section helps you to ascertain how well your investment worked for you. Fill in the left-hand column first to determine your profit or loss. Then complete the right-hand column to calculate your percent of profit or loss. Perhaps the most important part of the simulation is to analyze what you did right and what you did wrong in choosing your stock. The whole idea is to learn from the simulated transactions and avoid losing your money. Figure 17.6 shows how the Profit or Loss Percentage section would be filled in for Amrep.

Writing down all the details of your particular investment is a great educational experience. It also makes it easier to review your buy and sell transaction and learn from it.

Stock Price Data Sheet

The downfall of many investors is not following the stock after it has been purchased. They will spend the time to analyze stocks to determine their best investment, but then will get lazy or too busy to follow their investments. Consequently, they miss some great profit opportunities.

☐   **RULE 12**   ☐

Follow your stock price so you do not miss major profit opportunities.

The Stock Price Data Sheet (a blank sheet is provided at the end of this chapter—see Figure 17.9) makes it easy to follow your investments. You can write down the stock price every day (which I recommend) or every week depending on how volatile the stock is. The top section includes a little background information on the stock, including the 52-week high and low and the price you paid for the stock. These three figures are important in analyzing when you should sell your stock.

The main body of the sheet allows you to write down the daily (or weekly) closing price and the fraction it is either up or down. At the end of the week (or month), fill in the difference for that time period. Keeping this record will show how the stock trades and will allow you to easily determine if you should sell the stock. The Stock Price Data Sheet

Figure 17.5 Sell Transaction

> ### Sell Transaction
>
> Date _3-8-91_   Stock Price _$6,000.00_
>
> Number of Shares _1,000_   Minus Commission _87.00_
>
> Price per Share _$6.00_   Amount Received _5,913.00_
>
> Why did you sell the stock? _Met projected profit in three weeks. Sold to take a quick profit._

shown in Figure 17.7 illustrates what the daily price move on Amrep may look like.

Figure 17.6 Profit or Loss Percentage

> ### Profit or Loss Percentage
>
> Amount Received _5,913.00_ (Profit) or Loss _2,089.50_
>
> Minus Purchase Price _3,823.50_ Divided by Purchase Price _3,823.50_
>
> (Profit) or Loss _2,089.50_   Percent (Profit) or Loss _55%_
>
> What did you learn from this transaction? _If you can make 50 percent on your money in three weeks, take your profits._

Figure 17.7 Stock Price Data Sheet on Amrep

Stock Price Data

52-Week High	Low	Company Name	Date Purchased	Price per Share
8.38	3.25	Amrep Corp.	2-15-91	3.75

Day or Week	Price per Share	Up or Down	Day or Week	Price per Share	Up or Down
1	3.75	bought	21		
2	4.00	+1/4 250	22		
3	4.25	+1/4 250	23		
4	4.125	-1/8 -125	24		
5	4.25	+1/8 125	25		
Change	+1/2 500		Change		
6	4.375	+1/8 125	26		
7	4.375	unchanged	27		
8	4.25	-1/8 -125	28		
9	4.50	+1/4 250	29		
10	4.75	+1/4 250	30		
Change	+1/2 500	+1,000	Change		
11	4.50	-1/4 -250	31		
12	4.625	+1/8 125	32		
13	5.00	+3/8 375	33		
14	5.25	+1/4 125	34		
15	6.00	+3/4 750	35		
Change	+2 1/4 2,250 Sell		Change		
16			36		
17			37		
18			38		
19			39		
20			40		
Change			Change		

Selling Price: $6.00

Figure 17.8 Stock Record Sheet

Stock Record

Company Name _____

Address _____

City _____ State _____ Zip _____

Telephone Number _____

Exchange _____ Stock Symbol _____

52-Week High _____ 52-Week Low _____

Buy Transaction

Date _____ Stock Price _____

Number of Shares _____ Plus Commission _____

Price per Share _____ Purchase Price _____

Why did you purchase the stock? _____

_____

Stock Price Projection _____

Sell Transaction

Date _____ Stock Price _____

Number of Shares _____ Minus Commission _____

Price per Share _____ Amount Received _____

Why did you sell the stock? _____

_____

Profit or Loss Percentage

Amount Received _____ Profit or Loss _____

Minus Purchase Price _____ Divided by
                             Purchase Price _____

Profit or Loss _____ Percent Profit or Loss _____

What did you learn from this transaction? _____

_____

Figure 17.9 Stock Price Data Sheet

Stock Price Data

52-Week High	Low	Company Name	Date Purchased	Price per Share

Day or Week	Price per Share	Up or Down	Day or Week	Price per Share	Up or Down
1			21		
2			22		
3			23		
4			24		
5			25		
Change			Change		
6			26		
7			27		
8			28		
9			29		
10			30		
Change			Change		
11			31		
12			32		
13			33		
14			34		
15			35		
Change			Change		
16			36		
17			37		
18			38		
19			39		
20			40		
Change			Change		

Selling Price: _____

CHAPTER

18

How Much Have You Learned?

Winning Big with Bargain Stocks was written to help you become a wiser and more profitable investor. By investing the time to read and analyze this information, you have taken the first step. Applying this knowledge to your future investments will give you a more solid foundation for making smart investment decisions.

The book has covered diverse topics, such as how to find potential investments, how to analyze them, the positive and negative aspects that can affect a stock's profit potential, tips for buying and selling your stock for the best profit, locating the right broker for your needs, how to avoid scams and how the economy can affect the stock market. You have the information, now it is up to you to apply it.

This final chapter offers the opportunity to test just how much you have learned. The questions that follow cover some of the facts you should know. The page number in parentheses indicates where the answer can be found.

Chapter 1: Following Your Investment Dream

What are the 12 rules that make up the CHEAP philosophy? (p. 4)

Why are stocks listed in 1/8s? (p. 6)

How can you avoid falling into the greed/fear trap?   (p. 40)

Chapter 5: Analyzing Stocks Easily and Profitably

Explain the differences between fundamental and technical analysis.   (p. 42)

Why is fundamental analysis better, especially in a bear market?   (p. 46)

When you analyze a company, what information will you need?   (p. 47)

What are the five parts of the financial statement?   (p. 48)

What should you analyze in the annual report?   (p. 49)

What should you check in the 10-K report?   (p. 50)

Why is it important to get all the facts before you invest?   (p. 52)

What three key items can almost guarantee that a stock's price will go up after you purchase it?   (p. 53)

Chapter 6: Mastering Stocks under $10

What is a CHEAP stock?   (p. 55)

Why does the small investor need a higher rate of return than the large investor?   (p. 55)

Why shouldn't small investors buy high-priced stocks?   (p. 55)

Why do CHEAP stocks outpace the blue-chip stocks?   (p. 56)

What are three important points to remember when buying CHEAP stocks?   (p. 58)

How can you find CHEAP stocks?   (p. 58)

When analyzing OTC stocks, what are the recommended price spreads?   (p. 60)

Why are OTC pink-sheet stocks a poor investment?   (p. 61)

Why is it important to always check the bid and asked price before buying a stock?   (p. 62)

What are the three criteria for successful investing?   (p. 63)

GLOSSARY

accounts payable A liability reflected under the "current" section of a balance sheet. It may include the total of amounts due within one year for the purchase of inventory or other direct costs, general overhead expenses and other amounts owed.

ADR American Depository Receipt is a receipt in the form of a certificate for U.S.-traded securities representing stock in foreign corporations.

annual report The yearly financial statement of a corporation's financial condition. The report shows assets, liabilities and earnings, as well as a description of the company's operations — how it stood at the close of the business year, how it fared profitwise and other information of interest to shareholders.

ASE American Stock Exchange is ranked second behind the NYSE in most stringent requirements for listing.

asked The lowest price that is acceptable to a seller of a security at a particular time. Price that a potential shareholder would have to pay to buy stock in that security.

asset   Any item of value that is owned by a business, institution or individual.

balance sheet   A condensed financial statement providing a picture of a company's assets, liabilities and capital on a given date.

bear   Someone who believes the market will decline.

bear market   A declining market in stocks usually brought on by anticipation of declining economic activity.

bid   The highest price a prospective buyer is prepared to pay at that specific time for a security. Price that a shareholder would receive if he or she sold the stock.

block trade   A trade involving 10,000 or more shares of stock.

blue-chip stock   Shares of a company known for the quality and wide acceptance of its products or services with a steady record of profit growth and dividend payouts and a high probability of continued growth and future earnings.

blue-sky laws   The popular name for laws enacted by various states to protect the public against securities frauds. The term is said to have originated from a judge who asserted that a particular stock had about as much value as a patch of blue sky.

book value   Determined by the total assets of a company, minus liabilities and preferred stock. The sum is divided by the number of outstanding common stock shares.

broker   An individual who acts as an agent in the buying and selling of investments.

bull   Someone who believes the market will rise.

bull market   A rising stock market. Usually lasting at least a few months, bull markets are characterized by large trading volume.

capital gain or capital loss   The profit or loss difference between the purchase and sale price of an investment.

cash flow   An accounting term describing the positive or negative effect on cash generated from operations. It is the net income of a corporation plus amounts charged off for depreciation, depletion, amortization, etc.

certificate   A document proving ownership of a security. Usually, it is finely engraved with delicate etchings on watermarked paper to discourage forgery.

churning   A practice of overactive trading of customer accounts to generate commission income for the broker rather than to make a profit for the customer.

closely held corporation   Any corporation in which a substantial portion of the voting shares are held by a small number of shareholders.

closing price   Price at which a security trades at the close of the day.

collateral   Securities or other assets pledged by a borrower to guarantee repayment of a loan.

commission   The broker's fee for buying or selling a security.

common stock   Securities representing an ownership interest in an incorporated enterprise. Common stockholders have a residual claim on earnings and assets after all debt and preferred stock obligations have been met.

conflict of interest   A situation in which an individual who has control, influence or authority over a company may personally benefit from actions or decisions made by that company.

conglomerate   A corporation that has diversified its operations usually by acquiring enterprises in widely varied industries.

Consumer Price Index   Published by the Department of Labor, the index measures the prices of consumer goods and services.

convertible   A bond, preferred share or debenture that may be exchanged by the owner for common stock.

current assets   A company's tangible assets that are held in the form of cash or any other form that could be converted to cash within one year.

current liabilities   A company's debts that are due and payable within one year.

day order   A type of buy or sell order that is valid only for a single trading day.

debenture   A promissory note backed by the general credit of a company and usually not secured by a mortgage or lien on any specific property.

depreciation   A bookkeeping entry. Normally, charges against earnings to write off the cost, less salvage value, of an asset over its estimated useful life.

dilution   A decrease in the percentage of ownership in a corporation to an individual stockholder when more shares are issued to other stockholders.

discount broker   A broker offering only services to buy or sell securities. The commission is cheaper because he or she gives no investment consultation, advice, literature or other support.

discount rate   The interest rate charged by the Federal Reserve System on loans to member banks.

diversification   Spreading investments among different types of investments, companies, industries and risks.

dividends   Payments made by companies to their stockholder, usually from profits.

dollar cost averaging   A system of buying securities at regular intervals with a fixed-dollar amount, rather than purchasing a specific number of shares or units.

Dow   Usually refers to the Dow Jones Industrial Average, the most commonly used stock-market index.

earnings per share   The amount of net income earned per share of common stock after payment of dividends to preferred stockholders.

earnings report   Also called income statement, this shows a company's earnings or losses over a given period.

effective date   The date when a registered offering may be sold to the public.

face value   The par value of a bond, printed on the face of the certificate, indicating the amount the issuer promises to pay on maturity.

fiscal year   A 12-month business year chosen by an organization for tax and financial reporting. The fiscal year may end at any month.

float   Shares of a security available for buying or selling. Shares in the public hands as opposed to closely held.

forms 10-K and 10-Q   Reports filed with the SEC by all listed corporations. The 10-K is an annual report and the 10-Q is a quarterly report.

fundamental analysis   The evaluation of a company by studying its management, financial and competitive positions.

going public   Offering securities to the public for the first time.

Gross National Product (GNP)   A measure of a nation's total output. It is the value of goods and services bought and sold, including personal consumption, government purchases, investment in business equipment and the net difference between foreign purchase of American exports and domestic purchase of foreign imports.

growth stock   A stock with a record of rapid growth or the potential for rapid growth.

holding company   A corporation that owns the securities of another, in most cases with voting control. A holding company may be formed to manage and control several related companies.

hot issue   A security about to be offered for sale that has generated extreme interest and should trade above the public offering price.

hype   To promote a stock with misleading or inaccurate information.

inactive stock   A stock that trades a very low volume of shares. Many inactive stocks are traded in ten-share units rather than the customary 100-share units.

income statement   A financial statement providing a picture of the company's interim earnings. Income statements report total revenues, costs, expenses and net earnings from operations.

inflation   The economic environment in which prices rise, resulting in a decline in the buying power of the dollar.

inside information   Company affairs that have not been made public. It is illegal to use inside information on, for example, a takeover attempt or greatly changed earnings to buy or sell stock for a profit.

insider   An officer or director of a corporation, anyone who owns ten percent or more of a company's voting stock or an individual with inside information.

institutional investor   An organization whose primary purpose is to invest its own assets or those held in trust by it for others. It trades in high volumes, receiving discounted commissions for block trading.

interest   The payment a borrower makes to a lender for the use of the lender's money.

investment   Using money to make more money, to gain income or increase capital or both.

investment adviser   An individual who provides financial consultation. The title is used by financial planners, registered investment advisers and securities and insurance salespeople.

investment banker   Another term for an underwriter or any person or firm helping a corporation issue new securities.

investment company   A company whose sole purpose is to earn income by investing the pooled capital of many other investors in other corporations.

issue   Any of a company's securities or the act of distributing such securities.

junk bond   A bond with a speculative rating of BB or lower by Standard & Poor's and Moody's rating systems. The ratings range from AAA (highly unlikely to default) to D (in default).

leverage   The technique of using borrowed funds or special types of securities (warrants, calls) in an attempt to increase the rate of return on investment. While the rate of return using leverage is greater, the risk to the investor is also increased because the principal and specified rate of interest must be repaid.

liabilities   All obligations or debts owed by a corporation.

limit order   An order to buy or sell a security, if it is possible, at a specified price.

liquidation   The process of converting securities or other property into cash.

liquidity   The ease with which an investment can be converted to cash.

listed stock   The stock of a corporation listed on one of the major exchanges. To become listed and maintain that listing, a corporation must meet certain criteria.

load   The sales charge assessed against investors in mutual-funds, direct-participation and other investment programs. The load usually covers sales commissions and all other distribution costs.

manipulation   Buying or selling a security for the purpose of creating the false or misleading appearance of active trading. The creation of an artificial price movement, either up or down, to induce the purchase or sale of the security by other investors.

margin   Buying securities with a percentage of the purchase price borrowed through the brokerage firm.

market maker A dealer on the Over-the-Counter exchange who maintains firm bid and offer prices in a particular security by standing ready to buy or sell round lots at publicly quoted prices.

market order Order to buy or sell a security at the best available price.

market price The current or last reported price for which a security traded.

municipal bond Taxfree bonds issued by state and local governments.

NASD National Association of Securities Dealers is a self-regulatory agency for brokers and dealers in the over-the-counter securities business.

NASDAQ National Association of Securities Dealers Automated Quotations is an information network providing price quotations on securities traded over the counter.

net income The profits from company operations. Net income may mean actual income either before or after deducting applicable Federal income taxes.

net worth Assets minus liabilities. Total stockholder's equity in a corporation.

new issue The sale of a stock or bond that has not previously been offered by a corporation.

NYSE New York Stock Exchange is the world's most important and active investment trading market and has the highest standards for stock listing.

NYSE composite index The composite index of all stocks listed on the New York Stock Exchange, weighted by the number of shares outstanding and reporting the change in value. The index assigns a dollar value to that change to indicate relative movements.

odd lot A stock trade of fewer than 100 shares. Round lots are traded in groups of 100 or multiples of 100 shares.

offer The price at which a security is offered for sale. (Same as asked price.)

open order An order to buy or sell securities that has been given, but is not yet concluded. It can be closed in three ways: cancellation, execution or expiration.

option The exclusive right to buy or sell property or securities at a specified price within a specified time. Usually, an option has a much shorter time period than a warrant.

Over the Counter Securities traded among broker-dealers and not through listings on an exchange. Securities include those of corporations that do not meet the listing criteria of the NYSE or ASE exchanges, government and municipal debt securities and the securities of many financial-service companies (banks, insurance companies, etc.).

paper profit or loss An unrealized profit or loss on a security caused by the price either moving upward or downward from the investor's purchase price. Paper profits or losses become real only when the security is sold.

par value The dollar amount assigned to a common share by the company's charter. Par value has little significance as far as the market value of common stock is concerned.

penny stocks Low-priced issues, often highly speculative, selling for less than $1 per share. Often used as a derogatory term. A few penny stocks have grown into exceptionally high-quality companies.

pink sheets A publication listing the bid and asked prices as well as the market makers of Over-the-Counter securities that do not have a stock symbol. Pink-sheet stocks can be very speculative, with large spreads between the bid and asked prices.

portfolio An individual's or institution's securities holdings. A portfolio may contain bonds, preferred stocks and common stocks of various types of enterprises.

preferred stock   Like common stock, except usually without voting rights. However, specified dividends are paid to preferred stockholders before dividends are paid on the common shares.

price-earnings ratio   A stock's market price divided by earnings per share for a 12-month period. A low P/E ratio is considered relatively safe, but less likely to increase in value in a bull market. A high P/E ratio indicates greater risk and volatility.

primary market   The initial market for the distribution of securities. After the initial sale, they are traded in the secondary market.

profit taking   Selling a stock that has gone up in value since its purchase in order to realize the profit. Profit taking is often the cause of a downturn in the market following a period of rising prices.

prospectus   The official selling circular that all companies offering new securities for public sale must file with the SEC. The prospectus offers detailed information about the company's financial position, planned use of the new funds and the qualifications of the corporate officers, etc.

proxy   A signed authorization by a shareholder allowing someone else to represent him or her and vote his or her shares at the shareholders' meeting.

proxy fight   The attempt by a group of shareholders to obtain enough votes to replace a corporation's management or overrule it on specific decisions.

proxy statement   The SEC-required statement of information about the items being voted on, which must be given to stockholders when a solicitation for a proxy is mailed.

public offering   The sale of securities to the general public.

quotation or quote   The highest bid to buy and the lowest offer to sell a security at a specific time. If your broker gives you a quote on a stock as $1^{1}/_{2}$ to $1^{3}/_{4}$, it means that if you wish to buy stock it would cost you $1.75 per share; however if you wish to sell stock you would receive $1.50 per share.

rally   A sudden and unexpected increase in market value, either in the stock market as a whole or a particular industry or security.

random walk   A theory of market behavior that states that the price of securities cannot be determined, but is entirely random.

regional exchanges   Stock exchanges that serve distinct regions, such as Philadelphia, Pacific, Boston, Midwest, etc.

registration   Before a new security can be offered to the public, the security must be registered under the Securities Act of 1933. The company must disclose pertinent information relating to its operations, securities and management.

reverse split   The reduction of the total number of shares outstanding by reissuing shares at a higher par value. Usually bad news for shareholders.

rights   The opportunity (at the company's discretion) for shareholders to acquire new stock at a specified price and in relation to the number of shares currently held.

round lot   The basic unit in which stocks are traded. For most securities this is 100 shares.

Schedule 13D   A Schedule 13D must be filed with the SEC by any person who purchases or acquires five percent or more of the securities in any corporation registered with the SEC.

SEC   Securities and Exchange Commission is a federal agency with direct regulatory authority over the securities industry.

secondary market   A market in which securities can be bought and sold by the public, following an initial offering.

sell order   An order given by a customer to a broker-dealer to liquidate (sell) a security on the market.

shareholders' meeting   The annual meeting held by a public company to give shareholders a voice in company actions.

shares outstanding   The number of a corporation's shares that are owned by the public (including management) and not held by the corporation in its treasury.

short sale   A form of speculation in which the price of a stock is expected to decline. Securities are borrowed and sold and are later bought back at the lower price.

sinking fund   Money regularly set aside by a company to redeem its bonds, debentures or preferred stock from time to time as specified in the company's charter.

SIPC   Securities Investors Protection Corporation is a government-sponsored, nonprofit organization that insures customer cash and securities on deposit with a member securities firm.

specialist   A member of the NYSE who acts as a broker in the execution of orders and as a dealer by transacting for his or her own account. The specialist maintains an orderly market in the stocks for which he or she is registered as a specialist.

speculating   Purchasing high-risk, volatile investments with the hope of realizing large returns.

Standard & Poor's Corporation   An influential company in the investment area that rates bonds, collects and reports data and computes market indexes.

stock-limit order   An order to buy or sell a security when its price reaches a certain level.

stock split   Dividing a company's existing stock into more shares and reducing the price per share to improve the marketability of the shares. Also called forward split.

stop-loss order   An order to sell a security if a certain price is reached. Used to protect profit.

stop order   An order to sell at a price below or buy at a price above the current market.

street name   Securities kept in the name of a broker instead of the customer who actually owns the stock. This occurs when the securities have been bought on margin or when the customer wishes the security to be held by the broker.

syndicate   A group of investors who agree to raise capital to purchase the securities of an issuer. Also referred to as an underwriter.

takeover   The acquiring of one company by another.

target company   A company that is the subject of a take-over attempt by another company.

tax loss carryforward   A tax provision allowing losses to be claimed in the years after the loss occurs. Can be used to offset profits so less tax is owed.

tender offer   A public offer to purchase shares of a corporation from existing stockholders. The tender offer specifies a price and time period for the offer.

thin market   Term to describe either a single security or the whole market when there are very few bids to buy or offers to sell.

third market   Trading of stock exchange–listed securities in the over-the-counter market by nonexchange member brokers and all types of investors.

ticker   Instruments that display both the volume and price of security transactions worldwide. Nowadays, the display is usually computerized; years ago it was on ticker tape.

tip   Advice to buy or sell a stock made on supposedly "inside" information.

trader   An individual who buys and sells for his or her own account for short-term profit.

underwriter   Usually an investment dealer who agrees to buy all or part of a new-issue security from a company with the expectation that the security can be resold to the public.

unit   A minimum amount of common stocks, warrants or other securities that are accepted for trading on an exchange. New-issue stocks may offer a unit composed of various amounts of common stock, warrants or other securities.

uptick   A transaction made at a price higher than the preceding transaction.

volatility   A measure of price movement in a security, industry or entire market.

volume   The number of shares traded by either a specific security or a whole market for a given period of time.

warrant   A certificate giving the holder the right to buy securities at a specific price, usually within a particular time period. When a stock's price is higher or expected to be higher than the warrant's specified purchase price, then the warrant has a market value and is frequently traded.

when issued   An abbreviation of "when, as and if" issued. Applies to transactions made on a contingent basis, when a security is pending issue and made on the assumption that the issue will occur in the near future.

yield   The return on an investment expressed as a percentage of the current price.

INDEX